clean&simple

scrapbooking

contents

First, to my parents, for always encouraging and supporting my creative endeavors, and not freaking out that I didn't have the math skills to become a scientist or a doctor.

Secondly, to my family, Dan, Aidan and Cole. How I got this lucky to be hooked up with you wonderful, amazing beings, I'll never know. But rest assured—I'm counting my lucky, lucky stars.

Thirdly, to Stacy Julian. Thanks for calling me that one fateful day, and letting me be a part of your universe. Remember, don't ask me to jump off a bridge, or we'll both be in trouble.

Next, to Molly, my original favorite photo subject. I'm no fool to know that 25 years of friendship doesn't come around every day. I love you. Will this make up for the year I forgot your birthday?

dedication

d

And finally, to Jen, Lisa, Margie, Shelley, Suzanne and Tara. You've shown me how scrapbooking connects, enriches and uplifts people in ways they could have never imagined. I love you.

foreword

by Stacy Julian

I will never forget the day I saw my first Cathy Zielske scrapbook layout. My chin dropped into my lap and an audible sigh escaped my mouth. I had been looking for her, I realized. I knew in my gut if I could find what I called a "Pottery Barn" scrapper, we could send this amazing, rewarding hobby in a whole new direction—and open it up to a whole new audience. Cathy was my girl! Not long after our first conversation, I invited her to join our team for an editorial planning meeting. I had fallen in love with her classic, graphic style, and I couldn't wait to meet her in person!

As a graphic designer, Cathy is skilled in applying the elements of design—particularly color, line and typography. She is an amazing photographer, and she writes with ease in a conversational tone that immediately engages readers. As impressive as all of this is, none of it affected me like she did. When I met Cathy, she was gracious and approachable and kind. At a local scrapbook store, bombarded with questions, she was open and honest, completely focused on answering each and every person.

I knew Cathy was a talented scrapbooker; I learned that she's also a genuine teacher. This book is not about showcasing her talent, so much as it is about teaching you and building your confidence. Cathy's style is *Clean and Simple*. Cathy's heart is pure gold.

Take it away, CZ!

Stacy

Editor in Chief
Simple Scrapbooks Magazine

7

Introduction
when i got simple

You have to go back—way back—to the fall of 2001, when I naively walked into a scrapbook store for the first time, thinking, "Oh, I'll just pick up a few photo albums." Famous last thoughts.

My new hobby was born. The Mother Ship had called me home, and I knew what I wanted to do. See, for years working as a graphic designer, I dealt with clients who wanted to fit as much information on a page as humanly possible. Right from the start, scrapbooking would become for me a little slice of artistic freedom—elegantly spare and steadfastly uncluttered. I was determined to keep it clean and simple.

What I didn't expect when I started this little hobby, though, is how much I would adore it. I never pictured myself as a crafty kind of gal. And whenever I try to put my finger on what it is about scrapbooking that so rocks my world, it always comes back to the same thing: scrapbooking makes me happy.

I get to take pictures and tell stories. I get to celebrate everything in my world that is good, rich, and above all, real. I get to remember. In turn, I am constantly reminded of my lucky, blessed life.

The layout at left is one of my early scrapbook pages. I still remember when I finished it. And yep, it made me happy. But what I realize when I look at that page is that little has changed. Sure, I got a little more experimental with design and fonts. But the essence of what I do today was there at the start. Take a photo, tell a story, and make a clean and simple page.

And, be happy.

Here's to simple scrapbooking and all that it can be for you!

Cathy

AUG 2 2 2003

chapter one

simple starts

Some cardstock, a photo and some words…all the ingredients needed for a clean and simple scrapbook page! We're going to start with a random **sampling of simplicity.** No themes. No techniques. Just scrapbook pages, and a little sprinkling of simple scrapbooking philosophy.

Maybe you're new to scrapbooking and are looking for layout ideas to get started. Maybe you're a seasoned veteran who's looking to simplify. Maybe you're somewhere in between. Whichever category you fall into, I hope to give you **ideas that you can take and run with.**

If you've never tried a simple page, then here's your chance to see what it's all about. So grab a few sheets of cardstock and some "pictures and glue" and come along for the ride. A head's up: **This simple stuff could get addicting!** Consider yourself warned!

"It's just pictures, paper and glue."

—Tracy Miller

BIRTHDAY PHOTO SHOOT 1993 BY SKG

FRIENDS PARTNERS LOVERS BUDS DESTINED ETERNAL

F·O·R·E·V·E·R

what is simple?

Simple is three things. First, it's a philosophy, the driving principles behind *Simple Scrapbooks* magazine. Spend less time. Leave most of your photos in the box. Let go of creative pressure. Scrap non-chronologically. Get the idea?

Second, simple is a style. But within that style, you can have shabby chic, collage-style layouts as easily as you can have clean, graphic layouts. Simple is just less stuff overall. And for me, simple means that photos and journaling take center stage.

Finally, simple is an overall graphic approach—fresh, linear pages that tell the story as directly and clearly as possible.

Simple doesn't always mean a page is kicked out in 15 minutes or less. And simple definitely doesn't mean boring! When you start working with the "less is more" approach, a funny thing happens. You find that the possibilities are endless.

play

For all the "Keep him out of my room!" declarations, and the "Aidan hit me" reports, there is nothing more beautiful that the two of you playing together. I had often wondered how the two of you would get along. Would you be too different to enjoy the same things? Would you constantly be at each other's throats? As it turns out, yes, you are occasionally at each other's throats, but the funny thing is, you are both so similar in so many ways, that when it's working, it really works. You make up crazy games, you put on elaborate performances and you pretend to travel on amazing journeys to anywhere. Sometimes it can be as simple as running through the hose on a hot summer's day. But somehow you seem to know that having each other is going to turn out to be a really good thing.

AIDAN & COLEY, SUMMER 2002

Dream

July 2002

Love

hugs and kisses

8.03

you will never be in short supply

Simplify. I don't scrap every photo that comes my way. If I did, I'd feel overwhelmed and uninspired! I've become a photo triage specialist, determining which shots are most in need of scrapbooking, and starting from there. What happens to all the photos I don't use? Two words: photo albums. There is no rule in scrapbooking that says, "Thou shalt scrap every photo." Guilt does not belong in scrapbooking. Who's with me?

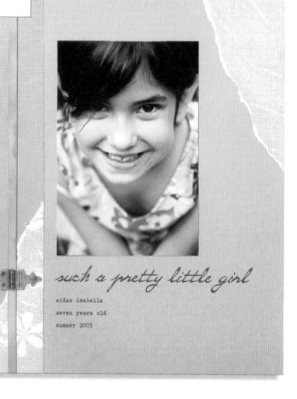

such a pretty little girl

aidan isabella
seven years old
summer 2003

just one photo?

Yep. Just one. Single photo layouts are the epitome of simple. Not only can you let a cherished photo shine, but look at all the leftover room to use for adding simple embellishments, trying new techniques, and placing titles and journaling.

I can tell a complete story with one photo, even if there is very little story to tell—as with the layouts on this page. I also love the challenge of finding fresh ways to highlight a single photo. It's clean and simple scrapbooking at its most basic.

cool
fresh
summer
august days
03sprinkler

One page or two? I create far more single-page layouts when I scrap. The benefit? I get more pages done and it helps me focus on what I'm really trying to capture. I have to ask myself, "Can I adequately tell the story with fewer shots?" And nine out of ten times, the answer is a resounding "Yes!"

Am I concerned that facing pages in my albums won't match? Absolutely not. If scrapbooking captures slices of life, since when does life line up so tidily?

It's really okay to have two pages side-by-side in your albums that don't match!

for now

january 2004

seven and four

respectively

you get along more often than you argue

you're not too old to take a bath together

barbies can be as fun as rescue heroes, and vice versa

you still give each other hugs and kisses goodnight

you'll watch the same shows

And for now, I love to see you share the bonds of siblinghood. I'm sure there will come a time when, even though the ties of the heart are still strong, you won't be wearing them on your sleeves. The pressures of growing up will try to put a dent in the armor of your relationship. It's okay to give into that. It doesn't mean you won't still be connected. Your connection is eternal. For now, know that you are one of each other's best blessings. 1.14.04

Make it your own! Customizing premade products to suit your individual tastes is where creative things happen. From using a premade frame as a mat (below), to mixing and matching laser cuts inside a premade window frame (right), you can put your own twist on any product.

premade simplicity

Tags, words, frames, ribbons, definitions…you name it, and those fabulous scrapbook companies and product designers are making it! There is a plethora of premade products just waiting to find a way to any given scrapbook page.

One of the best things about premade products? They do the work for you! Keeping it simple is all about taking advantage of the stuff that's out there for scrapbookers. And yes, credit cards are accepted at all major scrapbook stores.

I AM BLESSED. . . I AM BLESSE . . . BLESSE . . . I AM BLESSE

TO BE A WITNESS. . .

raison d'etre

There are times when I forget...because I wish I had a cleaner house, or furniture that matched, or kids that listen to everything I say, or a husband who jumps up and down with glee everytime I do a scrapbook page. I forget, but only for a second. These three people are what matter most. These three people are my reason for being. They make me a better person, and sometimes, a not-so-great person as well. A dichotomy I wouldn't trade for the world. Not for anything at all...

happy

1 lucky; fortunate   2 having, showing, or causing great pleasure or joy   3 suitable and clever

Go ahead. Be trendy! Simple style doesn't have to exclude trends, solely because they might not be "in" a year later! And just because I'm simple doesn't mean I won't try something at least once. If watch faces are in, I'll try them. If paper flowers and rub-ons are hot, you can bet I'll find some simple way to add them to a layout.

I could hold back the tide

with my Dad

by my side

Dad with me

got my Dad by side, with me

july 1998

simple trends

Being simple doesn't mean you can't try different techniques and approaches for creating embellishments on your pages. For example, I love the collage look. But sometimes the free-flowing nature of collage throws my linear self into a panic! My solution is to take a simplified approach. Keep it unaffected and stripped down, as in the layout at left.

Simplicity lies in the execution. You can try the most innovative, ornate-seeming techniques out there, yet still present them in a clean and simple way.

G B R D X W U N H X O
D S C W A V O H P J E
A V A R E B I R T H D
K V K T F N L R O J Q
B F E D O L M X E A N
Z E B G T J G O O D T
J B S I X T E E N R A
V X C A N D L E S J S
A V Z D R S T V S Y P
O Z I R E R G B C N K
T J A N U A R Y R B I
D F R Q B I C E C R E
Z V J G K I O U I B X
Y R Y E A R L X V C
F S M A G E C X I

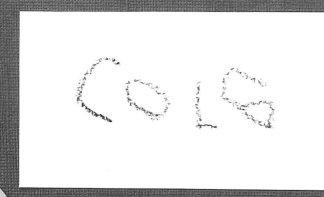

learn

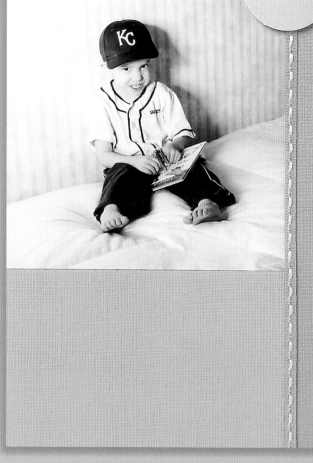

My little boy can write his name. This came as a complete and total shock to me, last week, as he's coloring away on some paper, and then says to me, "Mom, look—it's my name." Huh? When did he learn to do this? Am I not paying enough attention to the cognitive advances of my littlest one? So I look, and there it is, right in front of me, with an adorable backward "e" which is par for the course until you hit five or six. At daycare, they do a lot with letters and words. This is what I'm thinking as the thought strikes: "I did not teach him this! I am completely failing to stimulate his budding little intellect!" So today, being the scrapbooker I am, I gave him a sheet of cardstock and asked him to write his name. His comment after completion? "Oh Mom, I made a backward 'e'!" I will cherish that backward letter like heck. Before I know it, he'll be doing algebra.

readyandwilling

It's so hard to stand on the sidelines, ready, willing and able to play, and yet, it's just not your time. This was Coley's experience everytime Aidan had soccer games on Saturday mornings. At three, he was just a bit too young for the boy's league, and so he would stand impatiently on the sidelines just hoping to get that nod. You know the one... the one that says, "Hey kid, we could use a right wing out here!" To keep busy, he'd find whatever balls he could, kick them around, and try to get noticed by the big kids. Next fall, however, it will be a different story altogether. Our little guy will get to join the team, and the sideline days will be nothing but a distant memory of youth.

Words are as important as photos. Journaling provides a written record to accompany the photographic one. Feeling stumped for what to say? See Chapter 5 for ideas to get your verbal mojo flowing.

AUGUST '03

COLEY & THE SIEVE

THE LOVE AFFAIR CONTINUES... EVEN THOUGH COLEY IS WELL AWARE THAT THIS YEAR'S SIEVE IS PLAYED BY A DIFFERENT GUY, HE IDOLIZES HIM JUST THE SAME. AND THE COOLEST PART? SIEVE KNOWS COLEY BY NAME!

simple stories

One of the coolest things about scrapbooking is our ability to document the bits and pieces that make up life. No longer are we just flipping through photo albums, casually glancing at the photos as we go.

With scrapbooking, we have the opportunity to take those photos to another level—one with far more meaning and context.

You are more than a simple scrapbooker. You are a simple storyteller as well.

Player Name:
Aidan Zielske

Position:
Anywhere she can look cute.

Strengths:
Killer smile, good fashion sense.

Weaknesses:
Can't really skate that well.

Motivation:
Not falling down, and making
it around the rink.

Player Name:
Coleman Zielske

Position:
Goalie, sort of.

Strengths:
Knows all the words to
"We will rock you"

Weaknesses:
Can't really skate that well.

Motivation:
Total ice domination.

Player Name:
Daniel Zielske

Position:
Manager, coach.

Strengths:
Quiet intensity.

Weaknesses:
Can't really skate that well.

Motivation:
Making up for all the years he
didn't play hockey as a kid.

our very own minnesota
wild

event vs. moment

Do you scrap more events or moments? I am, by and large, a "moments" scrapbooker, and here's why: every event, small or large, is comprised of individual moments. Often I focus on one small detail and create an entire page devoted to that moment, rather than obsessing about getting the obligatory two-page birthday spread just right.

It's all about where your focus lies. Mine is on magnifying the moment. Fleshing it out, filling in the details, remembering the real-life elements that, truthfully, you couldn't make up if you tried. By doing this, I'm reflecting the richness that makes up my life.

Every event is full of these moments. How will you record the ones in your life?

treasure (trezh′er) 1. accumulated wealth 2. something of great worth

It's official—Dan and Cole have bonded. A funny thing
happend in the labor and delivery room. Apparently, Daddy
didn't feel that immediate bond when Coley was born.
Somehow, it was different than when Aidan made her debut.
It didn't take long for our sweet little Coley to win him over.
To this day, he will be tickling or snuggling or playing with
Coley, and he'll turn to me and say, "I think we've bonded."
It never fails to make me smile.

happy day

aidan's sixth birthday

Your birthday is such a happy day for several reasons,
the biggest one being it's our celebration of you joining
this world. So here you are, Aidan, six years old in the
blink of an eye. What lies in store for you during the
coming year? What new discoveries will you make?
One thing will remain the same: our love for you.

Form meets function. If you're going to mat a photo, why not make it functional? Simple metal hinges allow for hidden journaling.

to mat or not to mat?

One of the ways I've simplified my own scrapbooking is to forgo matting most of my photos. While matting is a great way to emphasize a focal-point photo, I look for other ways to make my images stand out (enlarging shots, or mounting them on foam tape, for example). More often than not, I dispense with the mat. Again, I'm trying to create clean and simple layouts. By removing the matting step, I'm one step closer to my finished page.

2003

glow

the setting sun at an iowa rest stop, and you...

your personality shines like a super nova,

with or without a light source.

does size matter?

I scrapbook in 8½ x 11, but that wasn't always the case. I started out 12 x 12 but quickly made the switch once I realized that I was never going to be able to cram a sheet of 12 x 12 cardstock through my ink jet printer. And while I realize there are larger format printers on the market, let's just say my husband wasn't buying it. Literally.

By using 8½ x 11, I've simplified my process. The page size is smaller, and I can run it through my printer.

There are benefits to all sizes. On 12 x 12, you have all that glorious space to work with, and you can scrap more photos. (With 8½ x 11, you have to maximize your space a little more efficiently.) And with even smaller page sizes, you can complete them at a more rapid pace, because there is less space to fill.

Space is simply space. It's all good. Choose your size. Or, mix it up. No one ever said you had to lock into one single format.

our

baby

boylie

taylor

Do you have a corner rounder in your stash? Have you pulled it out lately? Notice how by rounding the outside corner of each corner photo, it creates the feeling that the images are all just one big piece? For a different look to your page, round the outside corners of the layout itself, as seen on the facing page.

containing joy

are you caught up?

I just thought I'd ask, because I'm not. Not only am I not caught up, but some might say I'm laughably behind! With the exception of a few random theme albums, I have no completed scrapbooks. None. It's not for lack of trying, though. Well, actually, it is for lack of trying. Let me explain…

I adore this hobby. I love to create pages and put them in binders where I can still enjoy them. Or, I stack them in piles on my dining room table. For now, there is no order, no themes, and no chronology. The way I figure it, I have years to put things in order.

I have heard many a scrapbooker lament how "far behind" they are, or that they will "never be caught up." And I just want to grasp them firmly by the shoulders, tell them to take a deep breath and ask,

"But you're still having fun, right?" Scrapbooking is supposed to be a fun, stress-free hobby! When you say you're "behind," you're implying there's a time limit.

Turn off the timer! Enjoy the creative process. Be selective with what you scrap. Because really, are your kids going to want to haul away the 75 albums you made for them? It's the quality that will matter, not the quantity. I truly believe this.

I hope never to be caught up with my albums. I hope that scrapbooking is a life-long, ongoing process. I hope I'm 70 years old one day, still facing stacks of photos and making single page layouts that still make me smile when I'm done with them.

So are you getting it? Simple is as much about philosophy as it is about process.

a charmed life

every day, since she came along

8.99 aidan and daddy

chapter two
scraphic design

So you're a scrapbooker. It's official. If you've assembled your arsenal of supplies, you should be ready to sit down and create simple masterpieces, right? But do you ever sit there and think, "Great. Now what?"

Enter design theory: **if you're a scrapbooker, you're also a graphic designer.** And as a graphic designer, understanding the principles of design will improve the look and feel of every page you create, regardless of your personal style.

Design theory isn't rocket science, and shouldn't require hours of in-depth study. By understanding a few key principles and applications, your pages will come together more easily, and the results will make you say, "Dang, I'm pretty good." Scrapbookers should say that—and often. Let's dive in and get in touch with our inner designers.

a charmed life

"You know you've achieved perfection in design, not when you have nothing more to add, but when you have nothing more to take away."

—Antoine de Saint-Exupéry

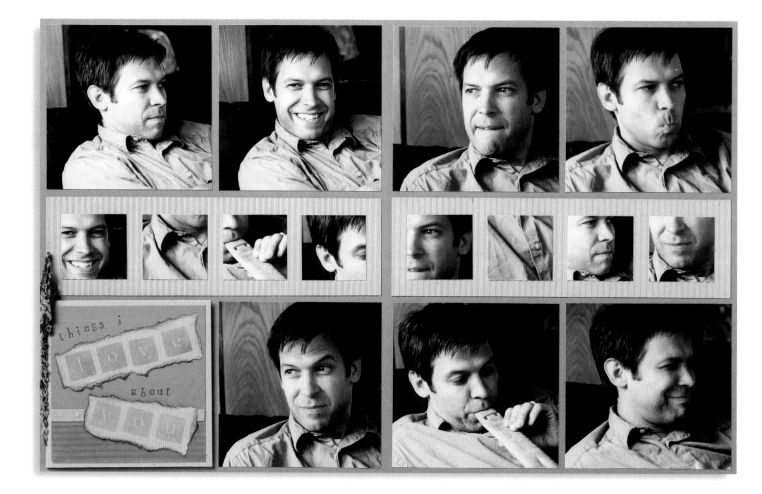

balance

Nothing is more important in layout design than the principle of balance. When balance is achieved, we feel good. When balance is off, we feel like something is wrong, but we just can't put our finger on it.

Creating balanced layouts involves two things: understanding visual weight and recognizing our need for order.

Visual weight is any element on a page that takes up space (photos, words, embellishments). Every time you place an item on your page, you subtract from the amount of space you began with. In a balanced page, space is accounted for in a sensible, identifiable way.

The need for order does not mean that the only way to achieve balance is through linear, static layout designs. Balance provides visual cues which help our brains make connections. It's not just about making pretty pages. A balanced layout just feels better somehow.

There are two basic approaches to creating balance on a scrapbook page: symmetrical balance and asymmetrical balance.

they say life...

- the extremely adorable, sing-song-y way you say just about everything, especially, "Ohhhh" and "Yeah"
- playing complete baseball games in the living room, complete with crowd noise and high-pitched screaming
- your dependence on Canada Bear to be able to fall asleep at night

- sneaking into Aidan's room to play with her Polly Pockets
- watching that scene from "School of Rock" more than 15 times in a row, then asking to watch it just one more time
- learning words in French and being so proud when you remember what they actually mean

...is in the details

COLEY 2002

◉ SCENES FROM A MELTDOWN ◉

Symmetrical balance is when you can draw an imaginary line down the center of a page, and what you have on one side you are repeating on the other. Think of it as mirror-image scrapbooking.

Symmetrical balance imparts a sense of stability. It tends to have a predictable order. All visual elements are balanced in terms of size and weight.

When you come up with a design for one side of a layout, or one page of a spread, you will then repeat that design for the second side or page. For a twist, try a modified symmetrical look: simply invert your first-page design on the second page, as in the layout above.

it makes me **happy**

IT'S CLEAN

IT SMELLS NEW

THE COLOR IS
AMAZING

THINGS ACTUALLY
MATCH

I'M NOT
EMBARRASSED TO
HAVE PEOPLE IN IT

THE SILVERWARE
DRAWER

THE OUTLETS ALL
WORK

I know—material things do not bring true happiness. But just look at my new kitchen! I cannot deny the fact that every morning, when I walk into this newly-renovated room, I'm filled with giddy excitement because holy Mother of Pearl—it's MINE! Things that are new and shiny make me happy. I think I appreciate them so much because they aren't commonplace in my everyday life. Don't get me wrong. I love the charm of my 85-year-old house. And truthfully, this kitchen doesn't necessarily blend with the rest of the rooms. But when I look at those gleaming stainless steel appliances, the warm cherry wood floors and the rich, light maple cabinets, I feel at peace with the world. So much for being a deep, non-materialistic person, huh? It's okay. I make up for it in other areas. Or at least that's the story I'm going with.

It's a love quite unlike any other—the bond between a father and a daughter. But even though I know that dads love their kids and vice-versa, I'm always blown away with emotion whenever I capture a glance from either of them at one another. There is such a deep love and connection that they share, and all you have to do to see it is look into their eyes. From the minute they first met, and each day since. You can just see the love in their eyes.

You can SEE it in their eyes

Aidan
and
Daddy

Asymmetrical balance is achieved by using elements with different visual weight. Whereas symmetrical design amounts to placing similar elements on pages in mirror-image fashion, asymmetrical design employs dissimilar elements in a looser arrangement to achieve the same goal of balance. Looser, mind you, not random.

Notice how a large photo collage (upper right) provides balance for the photo, title and journaling on the upper left page. Although the elements are different, they occupy roughly the same amount of visual space.

Accounting for space is the key approach to making an asymmetrical design work.

A little off-kilter. If you draw a dividing line down the center of the layout at right, you'll see that what is on one side is not a mirror image of the other.

Asymmetrical pages feel more energized, and they allow more room to play with design.

DYLAN

1991-1993

Dearest Lily.... you would have been 12 years old this month. An old dog, to be certain, but not an unconceivable age. You were supposed to be with me for the long haul, fulfilling the time-honored role of past, great MacDonald pets, who lived long, pampered, well-loved lives. You joined our little family in 1991. I so desperately needed a connection to my former life—something to remind me of home, and of family. And you were the key. It was before kids, and even before Dan and I truly figured out how to live together.

Epilepsy cut your life short at two years. I still question why an older, graying, slower-moving dog isn't sleeping at my feet as I write these words. Maybe God was short on Huskies. Here's to you, Lil, wherever you may be. Thanks for being my touchstone.

FRIENDS

The two-thirds, one-thirds rule

If you divide your layout into three imaginary columns, and place the majority of visual information in two of the three columns, you create an instant asymmetrical design.

SLIGHTLY CROOKED BANGS
PONYTAILS OF PERFECTION
FRESHLY SCRUBBED
ANTICIPATING THE BIRTHDAY PARTY
AT SHAKEY'S PIZZA PARLOR
ME, AT FOUR YEARS OLD

repetition

Another way our brains connect things is by looking for the familiar. Enter repetition. Repetition is a key principle in design theory. By repeating elements—approaches, sizes, shapes, you name it—you create a rhythm and flow to your layout.

Logical connections are made through repetition. Themes and moods are enhanced and supported. Repetition is probably the single best way to create a unified page.

Anything you put on a layout can be repeated. From the size of the photos you use, to the adorable little paper flowers you just had to buy at the scrapbook store. How many times or ways you repeat elements is up to you.

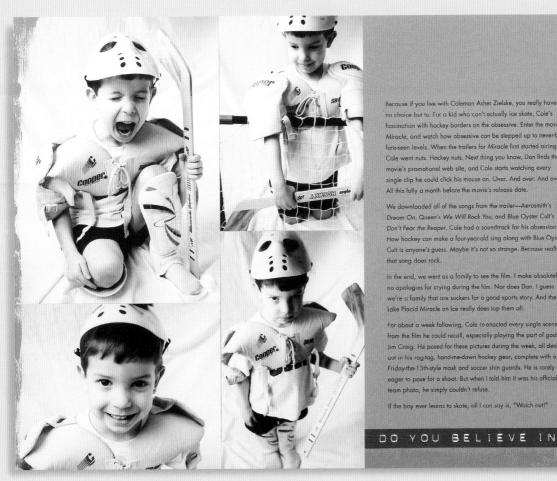

Because if you live with Coleman Asher Zielske, you really have no choice but to. For a kid who can't actually ice skate, Cole's fascination with hockey borders on the obsessive. Enter the movie, *Miracle*, and watch how obsessive can be stepped up to never-before-seen levels. When the trailers for *Miracle* first started airing, Cole went nuts. Hockey nuts. Next thing you know, Dan finds the movie's promotional web site, and Cole starts watching every single clip he could click his mouse on. Over. And over. And over. All this fully a month before the movie's release date.

We downloaded all of the songs from the trailer—Aerosmith's *Dream On*, Queen's *We Will Rock You*, and Blue Oyster Cult's *Don't Fear the Reaper*. Cole had a soundtrack for his obsession. How hockey can make a four-year-old sing along with Blue Oyster Cult is anyone's guess. Maybe it's not so strange. Because really, that song does rock.

In the end, we went as a family to see the film. I make absolutely no apologies for crying during the film. Nor does Dan. I guess we're a family that are suckers for a good sports story. And the Lake Placid Miracle on Ice really does top them all.

For about a week following, Cole re-enacted every single scene from the film he could recall, especially playing the part of goalie Jim Craig. He posed for these pictures during the week, all decked out in his rag-tag, hand-me-down hockey gear, complete with a Friday-the-13th-style mask and soccer shin guards. He is rarely this eager to pose for a shoot. But when I told him it was his official team photo, he simply couldn't refuse.

If the boy ever learns to skate, all I can say is, "Watch out!"

DO YOU BELIEVE IN MIRACLES?

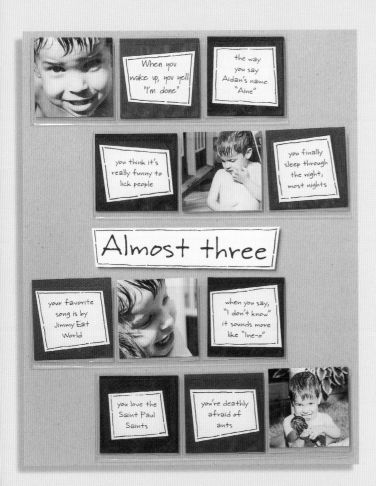

Repeat after me. Every time you repeat an element, you reinforce the design and the overall theme of your page. Additionally, repetition creates movement on a page by leading the eyes through the layout. Repetition works on levels we aren't even aware of. When you look at a scrapbook page, you may be thinking, "Oh, this is just lovely," but your brain is actually working subconciously to look for things that offer clues as to how a page fits together. By repeating elements, a visual path is provided that tells your brain how to process the visual information into something that makes sense.

The layout above has orange paint smears repeated, and the layout to the left simply repeats a pattern of three square shapes down the page. The simple repetition of elements ehances the unity of the pages, helping your brain process the information.

SUMMERTIME

There were some really great shots of you playing up at Chelsea Heights from this roll. For some reason, this photo—one in which you are nowhere to be seen—is by far my favorite. See, with this photo, I close my eyes and see you running like a wild banshee, digging in the dirt, screaming all the way down the winding slide, and going up to any kid you can find in an effort to make a new friend for an hour. Carefully lined up where the concrete meets the sand, this tells me my boy is happy and doing exactly what any four-year-old boy on a summer day should be doing—having the best time ever. Sure, I've got more photographic proof, but I think some things in this life are best left to the imagination. 8.02

A BATH TONIGHT

visual triangles

Anytime you take any element, repeat it three times, and place them in a roughly triangular relationship, you create what is called a "visual triangle."

Visual triangles enable the eye to make visual connections, which in turn creates the pleasant sensation of movement and flow in scrapbook pages.

If you were to take a pencil and connect the black titles on the layout at left, you would form a triangle. And if you connected the heart frames on the layout above (or the rub-on words, or the photographs themselves), you would again form a triangle.

Visual triangles reinforce your theme and demonstrate an implied design logic.

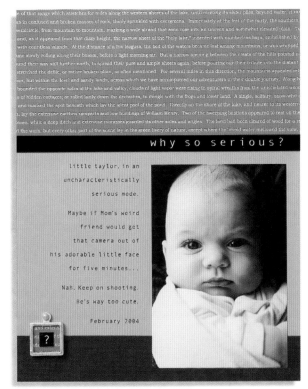

One, two, three. A black strip of cardstock at the top and bottom, combined with the black in the photo, form a simple visual triangle.

This Christmas at the farm, you had a glass of wine in your hand and I looked at you and said, "Uh, I hope you're old enough for that, young man," to which you replied: "I'm almost 22." Okay, stop—wait a minute! Did I miss something? You are 21 years old? That is crazy. When I moved to Minnesota, you were Dan's precocious little 9-year-old nephew. And now? You're 21! Despite my shock, there is one thing I can say, Matthew, and that is, you were at nine, you are at 21, and you have been at every age in between, one of the nicest, most engaging young men we have in our extended family. I was always so impressed at your ability to sit and simply relate to adults. I remember thinking once, "Well, maybe I would have kids if I could have one turn out this good." Because I think you have done just that.

emphasis

When you look at a scrapbook layout, can you tell what is meant to be seen first? If you can, you're looking at the principle of emphasis.

Emphasis is the spice of design. Why? Because it carries the power to engage, direct and inform the viewer. When you employ emphasis, you are saying, in essence, "Look here first. This is where the story begins."

Emphasis is a favorite convention of advertising designers. Take note of ads that get your attention. Some striking element typically stands out above everything else.

Does every layout need emphasis? No. But here are some layouts to show you when and how you can apply this principle to your pages.

Give me a man who can write a good letter and I'll follow him anywhere.

Our courtship began with letters. Lots of letters. We met in the summer of 1989. We kissed for the first time in September. But there was one glaring obstacle: distance. I lived down in Texas. He lived up in Minnesota. Aside from sharing astronomical phone bills, we shared…letters.

Every day, after returning from work, the first stop was the mailbox. And if I had mail, I would be swooning the rest of the night. Why? Because the man had a way with words. And not only could he craft a brilliant letter, he always chose the coolest stationery to put his words on. I'm sorry, but a man concerned with paper products is a keeper.

I think the act of writing solidified our growing relationship. It wasn't just the letters, but the process of taking the time to share, by hand, a part of ourselves with each other that really meant the world to me. I still have every letter Dan every wrote me. They reside in a tattered old vintage briefcase, carefully tucked away in my closet. Every now and then, if I'm blue or need any other reason in the world to remember how lucky I am, or how much I am loved, I open that old suitcase, and smile.

letter writin' fools

Have you met Mr. Square Punch? Next to repositionable adhesive, one of my favorite scrapbooking tools is my jumbo square punch. Creating small crops is a snap, allowing a focal point to stand out quickly. And a quick tip? Flip the square punch over, slide your photo in, so you can see the image through the opening, and punch. Quick and easy!

goalie always
seems
like a good idea...

until you get out there and realize that a) it's unseasonably cold, and b) all the action is down at the other goal. The result: soccer ends up being a bit boring. Not to worry! Aidan still manages to have fun during her second year of soccer, especially since this year, she and Nicollette managed to get on the same team (thanks in no small part to a little quick thinking on the part of Mom!) So if ever they tire of the riveting pace of the game, they can still find a million things to giggle about, while the ball just passes them by. SEPTEMBER 2002

Drama is good! When you exaggerate any element of design, but particularly emphasis, you create visual tension. Relax, this is a good kind of tension. Having one image large and others much smaller creates a visual drama on your page. There is a dynamic interplay between the large photo and the small photo. Here, the outsized shot grabs your attention. The smaller one supports the journaling directly.

I AM CONVINCED THAT DAN CAN DO
ANYTHING

3:33.12

Anything. You name it, and I'm absolutely convinced he could do it! At 38, in the best shape of his life, Dan ran his first marathon, along with Jonathan, and not only completed it in fine fashion, but with a very respectable first-effort time! I for one cannot really imagine what it's like to run for three-and-a-half hours, but that's exactly what he did!

We saw both he and Jonathan pass at the 13-mile mark, where Aidan leaned out to hand Daddy a PowerBar Gel, and I screamed at the top of my lungs as he was running away, "I love you, honey!" which got a chuckle from the crowd.

Dan has been training for this race, several times a week, for the past four months. He was prepared, both mentally and physically. Even though it was a glorious day in Rochester, it was sunny the whole time, and it did get a bit toasty for the runners. But Dan just doesn't complain. He takes the weather as it comes, and just keeps on running.

I was so overcome with pride when he crossed the line—he was so jubilant and happy! It made me cry, I think, not only because of how proud I was, and how proud he was, but that I looked at him and realized he can do anything—anything he sets his mind to. He is not only inspiring to me because of this accomplishment, but it simply mirrors every other aspect of his life—discipline, dedication and determination. As a man, a husband, a father, and now, a marathoner—he's all money, baby! Daniel Ezekiel Zielske, in a word, you rock!

3:33.12

MED-CITIES MARATHON   MAY 2003   26 MILES, NO SWEAT

The good news about focal-point shots. I love a good photo as much as the next scrapbooker, but the coolest thing about focal points is that the image you choose doesn't have to be the most killer photo of the bunch. Rather, select the shot that best captures the essence of the story you're telling. And then, play it up. Now, my husband crossing the finish line of his first marathon is obviously a focal point natural. However, by working with another photo, I created the layout at right which has a different focus altogether.

It all boils down to what best supports your story. You have all the control in the world, so when you decide what photo best tells your story, play it up.

MED-CITY
MARATHON 2003

A LITTLE HELP

She was so excited, and so ready...I mean, it's not everyday that your daddy runs a marathon, right? Maybe she didn't really grasp what it means to run for three-and-a-half hours straight, but that didn't stop her from taking her role seriously: the handing off of the Power Gel at the 13-mile point. Look at her...carefully keeping one foot planted on the grass while stretching her little arm as far out as she could. And the smile on Dan's face...hard to tell who was prouder, really.

Grouping photos together lends a wholeness to what could look piecemeal. These images "hang" together, based on common lines and shapes, resulting in a unified look and feel. Take any one of the photos away, and the balance is altered.

a walk on the wild side

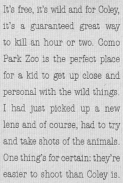

It's free, it's wild and for Coley, it's a guaranteed great way to kill an hour or two. Como Park Zoo is the perfect place for a kid to get up close and personal with the wild things. I had just picked up a new lens and of course, had to try and take shots of the animals. One thing's for certain: they're easier to shoot than Coley is.

coley hangs with the wild things
at como park zoo
september 2002

unity

Unity is the embodiment of Gestalt Theory, which states that the whole is greater than the sum of the parts. How you view the page is entirely dependent upon how unified the piece is.

Remember the old song from Sesame Street, "One of these things is not like the others"? That's not something you want people to say when you're striving to create a layout with unity.

That said, all of the principles up to this point are really springboards for unity. Design principles overlap and support one another. And unity is really where it all comes together.

Unity is the result of a well-balanced page which employs repetition of elements—shapes, colors, embellishments—to tie a layout together.

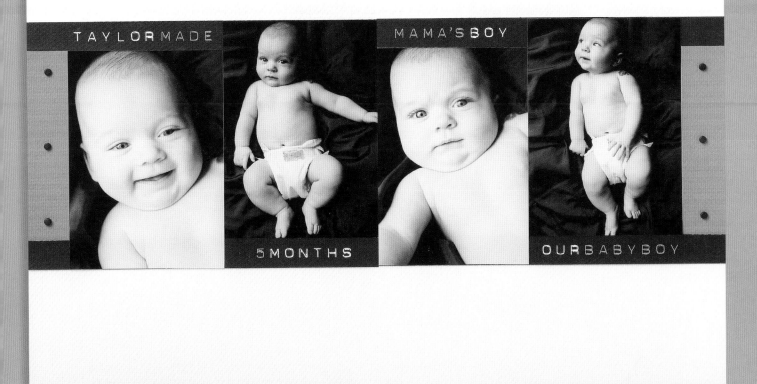

TAYLORMADE

MAMA'SBOY

5MONTHS

OURBABYBOY

1967   1969

1971   1977

IN DOG YEARS

Thank God my parents loved dogs. And thank God my parents raised me, side-by-side, with a small, but wholly memorable crew of canine companions. Thank God my mother didn't have issues with accumulating piles of dog hair, or furry people sleeping on beds. | Being raised with dogs made me a better person. They taught me how to listen, how to play, how to truly relax and how to get insanely excited over the simplest things in life. And they taught me the meaning unconditional love like nothing else. | Thank God, that my parents loved dogs.

It's good to belong. Anytime elements on a page have a direct relationship to one another, you create a unified feel. The layout above uses repetition and symmetry to create a unified link between the two pages.

Grid work. Designing on an imaginary grid is a shortcut to a unified page. When you align your photos on an imaginary axis, either vertical or horizontal, you are using a grid approach. In taking this approach to layout design, pay attention to the space between all "touching" edges. Equal space creates a more balanced, purposeful feel.

Open space directs you to focus on the photos and the journaling. Beyond that, space can trigger a curiosity as well. What is this layout about? Does the open space invite you to read on?

Among the numerous definitions in the dictionary of the word "thing," the one I relate to most when defining my favorite "thing" is: something (as an activity) that makes a strong appeal to the individual: forté. And as a noun, things don't get any more cherished than my camera. My camera is a mirror to the world as I see it, and sometimes, even as I thought I saw it, but was somehow mistaken. It's a doorway to magic and art, allowing me to somehow feel a justified connection to the world of art at large. It allows me to record and remember, laugh and lose my breath, if only for a second. It makes my hobby a joy and gives me a creative outlet I never knew I needed so strongly. Sure, I have other favorite things—my computer runs a tight second. But if I was allowed only one "thing" to take with me through the rest of my days, the Nikon would be my choice. (That, and a truckload of film, of course, to keep us company!) It is most certainly my favorite thing.

space

In a world of visual stimulation that bombards our senses, space is a quiet, welcoming invitation. Rather than demanding our attention with competing, often extraneous information, space lures us into the viewing experience with tantalizing restraint.

Space doesn't mean you must put as little as possible on a layout. Rather, by paying attention to space in both large and small amounts, you can invest your page with esthetic appeal.

Advertisers understand the value of space. Page through a magazine. Which ads stand out? More than likely, the ones featuring single product shots and lots of space. Engage your viewers. Invite them in. Sell them on your layout. Do it with space.

another year of joy, creativity, stress, happiness, discovery, humdrum, beauty, imagination, laughter, lunacy, genius and love.

38

family portrait 2003

PHOTO BY CHRISTOPHER M. WURST

For all the wonderful photographs that reside within the pages of my scrapbooks, or on the walls of my home, there is one subject that is sorely lacking—the family portrait! We are not a family portrait kind of family. In fact, we have never had an official family portrait taken. I suppose it's because I'm a bit of a photo snob, and never feel those Pro-Ex kind of pictures look all that good. However, it still doesn't solve our lack of family shots problem. What usually happens is this: we go to a family function, pose hastily for a shot, and get a copy of it sometime later. This shot is a prime example of our typical family shot: Aidan's hair is covering her face, Coley isn't even bothering to look into the lens or smile, Dan looks dark, and me, I end up looking washed out compared to Dan. Sigh. But maybe there is a value that I'm not quite seeing. A real-life quality that reminds me not every photo is a photographic work of art, but that a snapshot still carries with it the memories, the love and the connection of family. Yeah, okay… I like the sound of that.

Breathing room. Your page doesn't have to be empty. Even on one that is full of visual and written information, you can find ways to include space. The layout at left has a large journaling block, but by leaving the lower left open, as well as the upper left next to the stamped title, there is space that provides balance for the other elements, as well as providing a little breathing room for the viewer.

Let go of the notion that you have to fill every open space on a layout. The next time you're creating a page and you have some open space about which you're wondering, "Should I put something there?", just walk away and let it sit for awhile. Sometimes, you'll come back and realize the open space is perfectly fine.

The rush to buy gifts, decorate the house and bake endless cookies for Santa (or purchase them, if you're me) has come to a welcome end. It's not that I'm a Scrooge by any means, but my hope is always that my family will remain focused on the true meaning of the season. It's our night of traditions, which include an early church service followed by a steak dinner at whatever restaurant we can find that's open.

The Night Before Christmas
Clement C. Moore

believe

Christmas 2003

But the most memorable thing this year was Coley's race to hit the hay. After dinner, we decided to check on Santa's progress at the Norad web site, which features live radar tracking of St. Nick's progress. When I told Coley, "Wow, Santa is already in New York! That's only an hour behind us," he freaked out and ran to his room, saying, "No stories for me! I have to go to bed now. Everyone be quiet!" And I swear, he willed himself to sleep in less than five minutes. After Aidan was asleep, we finished wrapping some presents, had a visit from Laura and Larry, and managed to catch the final scene of "It's a Wonderful Life," which left us both sufficiently weepy. Then it was off to bed, to await the magic of morning. Indeed, all was calm and bright.

Pay attention to margin space. The above layout feels unified because of the common space between and around elements. Always pay attention to the space around your photos, your journaling blocks and your titles. Additionally, look at the space relationships of those elements to the margins of the actual page. Here, the margin space is the same on all four sides.

Trapped white space is when you have any area of space on a layout that has no direct relationship to the edge of the page. Space on a layout needs a place to go, and that place is a direct path off of the layout. When you trap space, it is boxed in—constrained in a way that visually makes no sense. Before you adhere your elements to the cardstock, look for areas of trapped space and see if you can either fill them or move elements around to eliminate them.

Graphic designers avoid trapped white space at all costs. It detracts from the flow of a layout. And good layouts are all about flow. The bottom line: space is good; trapped space is not good. Don't let good scrapbook pages fall into the trap!

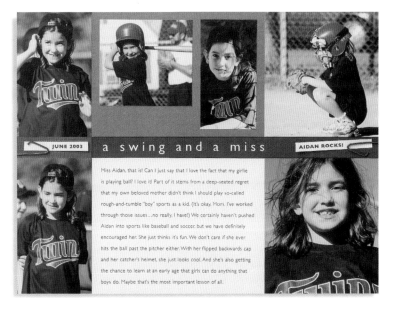

Free the trapped space. Can you see the boxed-in area of empty space on the layout above? This is trapped space. You can either move pictures around to eliminate it, or put some small embellishment in the space. On the layout below, I simply filled in all the space with photos. Problem solved!

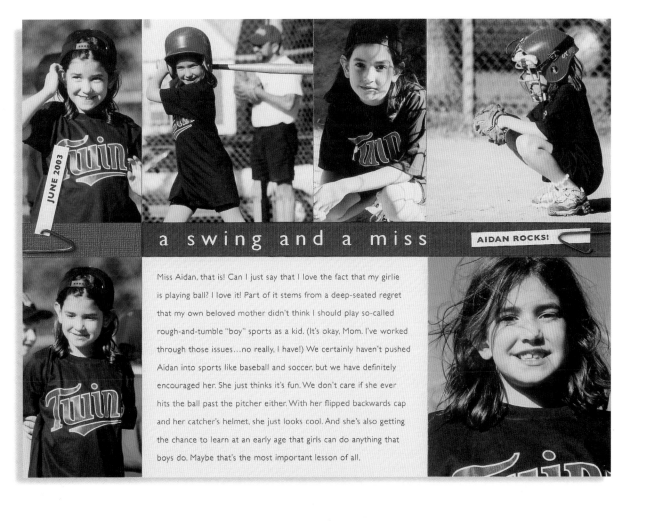

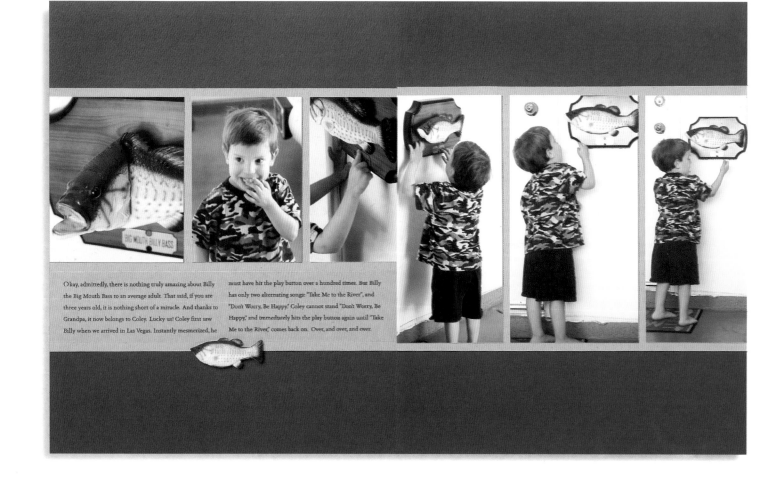

Okay, admittedly, there is nothing truly amazing about Billy the Big Mouth Bass to an average adult. That said, if you are three years old, it is nothing short of a miracle. And thanks to Grandpa, it now belongs to Coley. Lucky us! Coley first saw Billy when we arrived in Las Vegas. Instantly mesmerized, he must have hit the play button over a hundred times. But Billy has only two alternating songs: "Take Me to the River", and "Don't Worry, Be Happy." Coley cannot stand "Don't Worry, Be Happy," and immediately hits the play button again until "Take Me to the River," comes back on. Over, and over, and over.

in living color

Color is big. It's scientific. It plays a huge role in the overall impact of any scrapbook page. And there are tomes of information on the topic. I only have a few pages...

Look to your photos. Your photos will give you the color direction you need. Simply find a color you'd like to play up, and choose cardstock accordingly.

Get a color wheel and use it to create color schemes. Complementary, analogous, triadic—they're all there, laid out for your scrapbooking color selecting pleasure.

If you want your subject to stand out (**positive emphasis**), choose a color similar to something she's wearing. If you'd like the background colors to stand out (**negative emphasis**), select a color that matches the background.

Look to your color wheel. A color wheel is an invaluable tool for selecting colors. Once you've picked your main color, then you can make choices based on what type of color scheme you'd like to work with.

The facing page highlights four basic color scheme approaches to try.

common schemes

pure (pyoor) 1. free from anything that taints

GR8

little e·m

wonder

Monochromatic: varying shades or tints of a single color. One of the simplest approaches.

Analogous: any two to four colors that sit next to one another on the wheel.

SUPER LOUD

Subtlety is not one of your finer points. And this is not a bad thing. Bottom line? You're loud! Really loud. It comes in the forms of a) rocking out and making all accompanying sounds, b) the high-pitched scream that could likely break glass and c) the effusive way you express yourself on a daily basis. Like I said, it's not a bad thing. But occasionally, earplugs would be nice.

Complementary: colors that sit directly opposite one another on the color wheel.

friends

Triadic: any three colors that sit at a three-point triangle on the wheel. Primary colors are more muted.

guides for color

Color proportion. How much of each color you use on your pages can greatly or subtly alter their effect. A great rule of thumb for creating layouts with color balance is the gallon/pint/ounce approach.

The dominant color is the gallon amount. This color is frequently the main background cardstock in your layout. The secondary color is the pint amount. Use this to create journaling blocks, or smaller areas of background. The accent color, the ounce amount, could be as simple as some embellishments, or the mats you place around your photos.

Value. Value refers to the intensity of the particular hue. When you add white to any color, you are creating a lighter value, called a tint. When you add black to any color, you are creating a darker value, or a shade.

When you choose cardstock colors of similar value, you create a cohesive color feel. The layout at right uses complementary colors, red and green. However, the red and green are both shades, which add a richer, more elegant feel than if they were directly in the mid-range, which would feel more like Christmas red and green.

Don't be afraid to mix values as well. A rich red also works with a pale green, and vice versa.

Color balance A gallon of blue, a pint of white (in the patterned paper) and an ounce of green (in the ribbon).

Valuable Traditional Christmas colors such as red and green take on new life above.

celery & hot pink   orange & periwinkle   brown & pink

orange, olive & blue   any monochromatic combination

natural or kraft plus
absolutely anything

black plus anything

My favorite color combinations

Every scrapbooker eventually decides which colors are his or her favorites to work with. When you find those colors, keep on using them. I have a thing for celery green, orange and blue. Sometimes I think, "Hmmm…maybe I should give them a rest."

When you work with colors you love, though, your pages will be more inspired. Of course, sometimes that orange is going to clash with your photos. In that case, use your common sense to go a different route. Or, convert the photo to black and white and bring on the orange. Part of the reason I scrap black-and-white photos so often is the freedom of choice I then have with color.

A final word of advice: when in doubt, go with a monochromatic theme. It's safe, and it allows your photos to shine.

fyoosh:/fee-yoush
sincere relief; as
close one"; 2. a
ielske. 3. just
Aidan's pe

fyoosh
aidan's new word

There is a new addition to Aidan's ever-growing personal lexicon, which includes the unforgettable *potch*—as in "to potch something down"—and the charmingly accurate *bince*—as in, "I'll have a bince more of the spaghetti, Mom." Enter *fyoosh*. A word which has cropped up with moderate frequency during her seventh year. Apparently, *fyoosh* is a statement of relief and light disdain, originating from the words *phew* and *sheesh*. Will this word ever catch on and become a harbinger of seven-year-old culture, much like the term *way* emerged among teens who saw *Wayne's World*? Who can really say. Chalk another one up to Aidonics. We're just glad we can still understand her lingo. Because really, you never know what crazy word will be waiting around the cornizzle.

"I DON'T HAVE TO EAT IT? FYOOSH! I HATE BEEF BOURGUIGNON!"

chapter three
talk to me

I love to write. Since I was nine years old, I've harbored grand illusions of becoming a celebrated novelist. Unfortunately, many writing instructors have told me, "Uh, Cathy…why don't you **try the design department?**" Despite the fact I was never able to make my career as a writer, it didn't stop me from indulging in yet another passion. I have kept journals throughout the years, covering all the highs and lows of my life. No, it's not the great fiction I'd dreamed of, but I think it's even better. It's real life.

Enter scrapbooking—**the perfect outlet** for any writer, frustrated or otherwise. You can say whatever is on your mind, and no one will grade it, or judge it, or tell you it isn't good enough. Your audience consists of those in your innermost circle, and unless they're English professors, no one is going to focus on your lack of punctuation skills. No one is going to tell you to "try the design department." All they'll see are little bits of your heart and soul shining through.

You have to understand that as a scrapbooker you are a storyteller. Your stories are the most important thing you have to share. You don't have to be perfect. You just have to write. Don't let the pressure of journaling hang you up.

"Please talk to me. Won't you please talk to me?"

—Peter Gabriel

That slide was every mother's worst nightmare—a monolithic stairway to doom, or at the very least, a trip to the ER with seven to nine stitches required. And yet, you climbed up the 20 foot ladder, threw a foot over the edge of the slide and screamed with delight the whole way down with nary a scratch. One disaster averted. One heart rate returned to normal. I don't know if I'm ready for what's around the next corner, buddy. I only get one you. Keeping you safe is priority number two. Number one? Well, that's an absolute given. So if I ask you to swim in the shallow end, or hold hands in the parking lot, it's not because I think *you're* not ready…

not ready

MAY 2 2 2003

the problem

You've got these great shots of the kids at the park on a glorious summer day, risking their lives on the playground equipment, giggling and simply being the glorious little things that they are. And you, being a good scrapbooker, snap away.

Why is it, after you develop the pictures and sit down to scrapbook, that the words just won't seem to come? Why does if feel forced? You can design a strikingly beautiful page, and yet you don't really have a clue as to where to start with the journaling.

Relax. I believe writing seems hard because we were taught that it has to be formal and perfect. And you know what? It just doesn't. I propose that a far more casual, conversational approach can give a boost to your writing, increase your confidence, and allow you to get closer to your authentic writer's voice. Plus, it'll be more interesting to read.

Let's explore some ideas to get to the heart of what you are really trying to say. And no, it doesn't have to be philosophically deep every time!

kind

cool

silly

funny

true

my friend tara

Use premade word tiles as seen in the layout to the left to create your list. Or, simply start your sentences with the same phrase as seen below ("You are…) and then fill in the blanks.

10 things

you are adorable
you are opinionated
you are creative
you are smart
you are beautiful
you are feisty
you are loving
you are imaginative
you are funny
you are my girl

make a list

Think you're not a writer? Well, do you grocery shop? If so, then you're capable of making a list. And if you're capable of making a list, you're officially qualified to be a writer.

List journaling is a fast and compelling way to capture more sincere sentiments about your subjects than, for instance, the following: "Aidan is a wonderful child. I'm so very glad she is my daughter."

We know she's wonderful, but do we know the concrete details as to why? Grab a photo, and write down five to ten things about the person in the shot. Write more if you like, but use that list on a scrapbook page with the photo. It's quick and simple, and it tells a "story" that's real.

the free write

Remember the dreaded "free write" in high school English class? You'd sit, pen in hand, scrambling to say something meaningful on the true nature of liberty in 15 minutes or less?

Free writing is actually a great tool for scrapbookers. Here's your challenge: select a few photos you want to scrapbook, a sheet of blank paper, and a pen. Or, sit at the computer if that's where you write best.

Now, start writing. Don't be unduly concerned about making perfect sense. Don't correct your punctuation. Don't edit as you go. Just write non-stop for at least five minutes. Go ahead and report the facts: who, what, when, where and why. Don't forget the sensory side of it: sights, smells, tastes, etc. The idea here is to blather on and on. (How often are you allowed to do that?) Just don't stop writing.

When you're done, assess what you've written. See if there isn't something that stands out as a journaling nugget, a key sentence, phrase or even a single word that genuinely captures the tiniest sliver of what you're trying to say. Use this as your jumping-off point. Or, feel free to use your free write word-for-word. The approach is designed to liberate you from your writing inhibitions and just get writing.

the day before Thanksgiving, and you guys decided to play native americans. Aidan, you asked for the face painting kit, and i think i groaned for a minute and thought, no i'll be a fun mom and cooperate. So then, Coley strips down to the buff, and puts on his swim suit so he can look more authentic. It was like 19 degrees out! Then Aidan, you made feather head band thingies, and you were all set. You amaze me with the way you have the ability to get along. Your creativity is a joy too see. I need to stop sometimes, and just soak in your kidness. And remember what its like to be 7 and 4, when your living room really is a tee-pee. And your imagination has no limits! I am thankful fo

thankful

I'm thankful for your imaginations. As I watched you prepare to celebrate your own, unique Thanksgiving—Native American-style—I tried to remember what it's like to live in a world so ripe with imagination. Where I see a couch, you see a canoe. And that sleeping bag randomly tossed over two chairs? A bona fide tee-pee. Every day, you offer glimpses into your little minds, reminding me of a small part within myself that has long since been buried beneath grown-up responsibilities. So thank you for showing me that it's okay to wear a swimsuit on a 19-degree day. And that some rolled-up Carl Buddig turkey meat and a can of Niblets is a feast for sure. I'm thankful I get to remember that stuff. Thanks to you. 11.25.03

Sometimes, free writing unclogs those stymied brain cells just enough to get a functional flowing of thought. Here, I didn't use my free write word for word. Rather, I saw it as an opportunity to jump-start the sluggish motor of my brain to figure out what I really wanted to say. If you want your writing to purr, consider this approach to warm up the engine first!

14 years

After 14 years, I still feel happiness and relief when you walk through the door after a day of work. After 14 years, I've learned to recognize when I've pushed things a little too far. After 14 years, sometimes I still keep pushing. After 14 years, I admire you more than any person I've ever known. After 14 years, I've accepted that we're never going to have a big enough room for a king-sized bed. After 14 years, we've learned to split the difference on the thermostat, pretty much. After 14 years, we finally have central air, which buys you at least another 14. After 14 years, I know that the whole soulmate connection isn't just idle talk. After 14 years, there isn't any person I'd rather just do absolutely nothing with. After 14 years, the inside jokes just get funnier and funnier. And after 14 years, I realize meeting you was the greatest stroke of love and fate I'll ever know. Thanks, baby. I love you.

verbal repetition

Just as repetition can be an effective design tool, so too can it enhance your writing. By repeating a key phrase or question, you inject a sort of journaling parallelism—rich with cadence and familiarity—into your writing.

Repeat any words or phrases you can think up. Above, I repeated the sentence starter, "After 14 years…" and then filled in the blanks. Try making "I love you because…" or "I'm thankful for…" layouts, using those words as your sentence starters. After five or six sentences you'll have a powerful block of text for your next layout.

All that remains is to find random photos that support the words you've written.

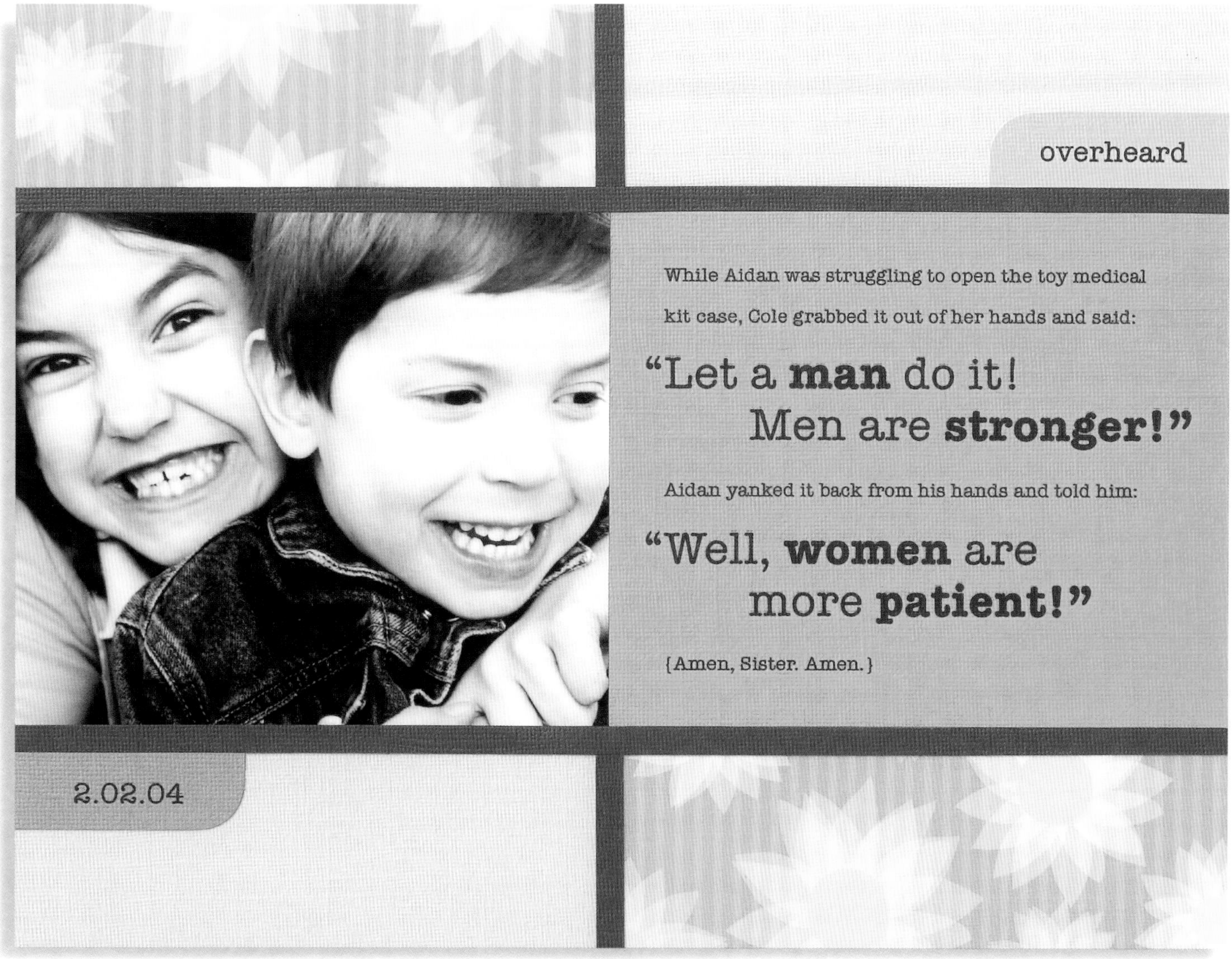

While Aidan was struggling to open the toy medical kit case, Cole grabbed it out of her hands and said:

"Let a **man** do it!
Men are **stronger!**"

Aidan yanked it back from his hands and told him:

"Well, **women** are
more **patient!**"

{Amen, Sister. Amen.}

2.02.04

can I quote you?

Kids say the craziest things. In fact, so do husbands, friends, mothers-in-law—you get the idea. When you're at a loss for what to say, let your subjects do the talking for you.

I'm talking about memorable quotes—not the inspiring, flowery prose of famous people, but the ordinary utterances actually spoken by the people in your life. If you get into the habit of jotting down what people actually say, you'll amass a collection of journaling gems that will lend surprising luster to your pages.

Keep a notebook handy. When someone says something, write it down. Use the quotes on a page as I did above. You may well paint a more accurate picture of someone's personality than paragraphs of journaling ever could.

Later, find a photo of your subject and create the page. Good point to remember: the photo doesn't have to be from the exact moment the words were spoken.

Coley's Question

"Mama, when will my heart die?"

You asked me this question yesterday as I carried you home from daycare, and I was completely taken aback. Instinctually, the first thing I did was hug you as tightly as your little body could withstand, and told you, "Oh Coley, your heart is going to live for a very, very, very long time." The next thought I had was why on earth you would ask such a question—where does something like this come from? You seemed satisfied with my response, and we went on with our day, although it was not an ordinary day in Minnesota. We had just learned that our state senator, Paul Wellstone, and his wife and daughter, had lost their lives in a plane crash.

Earlier in the day, I had a conversation with my friend, Margie, who said, "You never know when God is going to take you." This idea rang out in my head when you asked me your question. Part of me wanted to say that we never really know when this gift of life will leave us, and that there is no earthly explanation for the hows and the whys of why we go when we do. But your three-year-old logic would have simply pushed that idea aside, as you went about your enviably carefree day, playing baseball in the living room, and asking me to sing the "Star Spangled Banner" from start to finish before you assumed your position at catcher.

Later that night, I was watching "City of Angels" on television. There is a scene at the end when Nicholas Cage's character, after trading his life as an angel for that of a human, is mourning the loss of the woman he became human for, and asks another angel, "Am I being punished?" To which the angel replies, warmly, "You know that's not how it works." And then adds, "That's life." And all I could think was that after a day full of sad moments and questions, that I was supposed to see that.

So Coley, what I wanted to tell you is that your heart will never truly die. You and I, Daddy and Aidan, and all the people we cherish will one day leave this place, but our hearts will carry on in those we love. Your heart is going to live forever, long after the beat of your life ceases to be. You are eternal, Coley. God blessed, loved and eternal. That, is life.

10.25.02

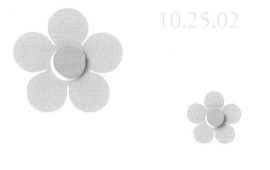

say a lot

There are times when a lot needs to be said, as I did in this layout. Real life often hands us our best journaling leads, if we halt long enough to listen. My son's question stopped me cold, and I knew I had to cease whatever else I was doing and start writing.

I think journaling has the power to illuminate and reflect both our perception and our reality. When you want to say a lot, by all means do.

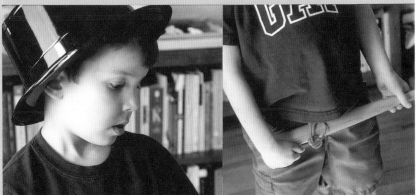

image is everything

First, you need the stance. Every rock guitarist from Hendrix to Prince has a stance. Secondly, you need a gimmick The black top hat and soccer shin guards will only add to the overall rock and roll mystique. Coley, we need to get you off the bat and onto a real guitar. There's a rocker inside you dying to get out.

march 2004

say a little

Don't be intimidated by the notion that you have to fill up a big space with words. There are times when you can say a little, and that's perfectly okay. The layout at right used a handful of sentences to tell a quick, simple story.

officially way too cute

{ in case there was any question }

say even less

Keep it even simpler with a title and one sentence. While I am the first to stand up and profess the importance of journaling, I also believe that you have to be realistic. For the layout at left, I didn't have a lot to say about my daughter. She just looked really cute to me, so that's what I wrote. End of story. Further, using a quote on a page is not taking the easy way out. If it means something to you, then that is all that matters!

a sure sign of **home**

the tire swing I spent hours upon hours in swinging.

the huckleberry bush we hungrily depleted each summer.

the "horse" my dad made for me on the fence.

the garden that barely yielded a thing, and when it did, Sandy, Pal or Bandit would eat all the tops off the vegetables.

the fence that Bandit jumped over, and was gone for an unbelievable two weeks before we finally found him.

the grass that died slowly but surely every year, only to be replaced with yet another segment of rocks.

the numerous slugs on a dewey morning.

the time a girlfriend and I were making a home movie and I laughed so hard I relieved myself on my clogs.

the theme park I created especially for my pet rock collection.

the hours spent in vain trying to get that Washington tan.

the woods behind the house that seemed to go on forever.

memories of my childhood backyard

what we know

we, of course, really means me there is
a fine line between inspiration and
obsessive-compulsiveness peter gabriel
rocks sometimes you will take really
bad pictures my children are brilliant
driving to the bus stop is much easier
than walking i have wonderful friends
you can never have too much sleep
money causes stress if you don't have
any technically, no one needs more
than one good pair of shoes time alone
is restorative there is nothing more
important than family music feeds the
soul oreos are a great creation

Have you scrapbooked...

- your first home?

- your favorite musical artist?

- your favorite modern convenience?

- your pet peeves?

- your worst habit?

- your biggest personal influence?

- your regrets in life?

- the things you know for sure?

scrap everything

Scrapbooking is a "dear diary" concept with photographs.
Do you remember what you wrote about on those pages
under lock and key? Probably everything.

Scrapbooking is your opportunity to revisit the diary
concept. You can and should scrap every aspect of your
life (within reason, of course). If you're just creating
pages about big events, such as birthdays and holidays,
you're missing so much!

Nothing is too mundane. Nothing should be off-limits.
Any detail of life has a richness, if we scratch beneath
the surface just a little.

A palace
for sure
235 CHARLES AVENUE

Frogtown. Not exactly the most glamorous
neighborhood name in St. Paul, but certainly one with
character. In 1990, Frogtown became my first Minnesota
home, when I left Texas to move "in" with Dan. The house,
a duplex actually, at 235 Charles Avenue was built in the
1880s. Dan bought the house from his Dad for $18,000.
His Dad had originally bought it to be a fixer-upper that
he didn't have time for. Dan rented out the upper unit to a
couple who fought frequently, until I moved in. His family,
in their 1990 Christmas newsletter, referred lovingly to
me as Dan's "special upper duplex tenant."

I remember several things when I look at this picture. The
mice. The halfway house for teenage boys directly next
door, where basketball was played from 7 in the morning
until 11 at night. The crackhouse across the street, later to

be cleared out and filled with more normal neighbors.
The occasional gun shots that rang out in the night. The
ancient electric air furnace in the upstairs unit. The
garage that was so scary I don't think I ever went in it.
The dirt walls in the basement that reminded me of a
scene right out of "Silence of the Lambs."

But then I also remember the good stuff. The way we
painted everything in fun colors. The deep claw foot
tubs I still miss to this day. The smell of the gas stove
when making a pot of tea. Dylan's friend "Merlin"—a
siberian husky who lived across the street that would
come over to play. The magic of having a place of my
own and sharing every day with the man I loved. It was
our first home. And in the words of Tom Waits, it was,
"a palace for sure."

freedom

in grapevine, texas

This picture was taken roughly two years after I'd moved to Grapevine, Texas, and it evokes everything I remember most about living in the South—namely, complete personal freedom.

I'd left Seattle at 19, mostly to escape all the emotional constraints—both perceived and real—in my life. I desperately needed to be in a place where I could start from scratch. I needed both physical and philosophical room in order to figure out how to just be me.

Was I afraid to relocate to such an unfamiliar place? Not at all. I'd had enough fear up to that point—fear of not being accepted, of not fitting in and of not being liked for me. The list went on and on. I felt as if I had absolutely nothing to lose. As it turned out, I gained an entire universe of self-awareness and confidence.

Not knowing a single soul was a blessing. It meant that each new person I met would have to take me as I was. I was free to choose relationships with people, not out of obligation, or past history, but out of mutual interest, desire and trust. I can't really put into words just how liberating that was.

I have so many fond memories of Texas: the wide, wide open spaces of the landscape; a part of town called Deep Ellum; the music of R.E.M., my constant companion during those years; getting into my car and just driving; and the two life-long friends I made there, Christine and Barbara. Christine would later introduce me to Dan, a lucky stroke of fate, and Barbara would become a true friend and confidant.

In this picture, I'm wearing a wig beneath the bolero hat, pretending for an afternoon to be someone different than myself. Looking back, I realize the best gift that Texas gave to me was the strength to remove the "wig," or any other false front I'd previously used to hide my true self from the world at large, and embrace the woman I saw in the mirror. And to tell her there was no one else I'd rather be.

It took me 21 years to find that resolution and I've been reaping the benefits ever since. So Texas, here's to you. Thanks for affording me the freedom to let me be me.

who are you?

Whenever I teach scrapbook classes, I always ask one question of my students: How many of you have created a page about yourself? I'm always surprised to see a couple of hands go up, shyly, almost as if they're somehow embarrassed to admit they have the audacity to scrap in such a selfish way.

But here's the deal: If you don't scrap about yourself, who will? No one on this earth knows you better than yourself! We spend so much time and care creating pages about the people with whom we share our lives, but oftentimes we neglect the source from which all of this creative effort flows. Ourselves!

silly me

self-portrait in 2002

It's not vanity, sister. When you create pages about yourself, you're giving an absolute gift to those in your life and to future generations. What I wouldn't give to look at scrapbook pages my mother could have made when she was my age! What was her daily life like? What were her dreams and hopes? Did I drive her crazy on a daily basis? Start today! Don't be shy. Keep it simple. Be like Oprah. Make a list about "the things you know for sure." It doesn't matter what you do, only that you do! Share your story. People will thank you.

Designer clothes will not make anyone cooler. So if I were you, I'd return those $75 Guess jeans as soon as possible.

You can cut your hair short. No, really! But just know this: your mother will never, ever forgive you.

Don't be a conformist. You have far more originality than you think.

You are beautiful. You won't figure this one out for years, and even then, you still won't always get it.

You will never be rolling in the dough, but your life will rich in ways that money truly cannot buy.

Adversity will show you a strength that you didn't know you had.

Do not, under ANY circumstances ever date anyone named "David." You'll have to trust me on this one.

All the highs and lows of the world will never change the bond you have with Molly.

hindsight is 20/20

20 things I would tell her if I could

Keep writing in that journal of yours. It will give you years of entertainment and reflection.

You are going to be a writer, but not in the way that you think you are.

Never, ever try to get a loose-curl perm.

You will never be a size 6, no matter how much you exercise or starve yourself.

Cherish your hometown. You won't live there as an adult, and you will miss it everyday.

You will meet your soulmate.

You were better off not going to the Sadie Hawkins dance with Jim Garberich.

You're going to have children one day. Yes, that's right—you.

Don't sign up for all the credit cards they're going to offer you your freshman year of college. I'm so not kidding here.

You will not look good as a red-head. And no, not as a blonde either. That's how you'll get the red hair in the first place

Never, ever try to get a loose-curl perm. I really can't stress this one enough.

Your charmed life will make you wonder when the rug is going to be pulled out from under you. Take a deep breath, and just go with the flow.

lighten up

Self-portrait pages don't have to be too self-consciously serious! Here's a journaling challenge: Find a picture of yourself from your high school years and make a list of things that you would tell that young woman in the picture, knowing what you know today.

I did this for my "hindsight" layout and found myself laughing out loud remembering the bad perms, the thought that owning Guess jeans would make me popular, and that my mother still has never forgiven me for cutting my hair short!

And beyond that, it gave me a chance to tell that girl in the photo some of the things she was dreaming would one day come true.

We had roughly 40 minutes to sit, bond, look at photos on T's camera, and hang. Just a quick layover at the Minneapolis-St. Paul International airport. Just a quick little soul injection. There is no earthly explanation how we got to be friends, when you really stop and think about it. Never lived in the same town. Ten years separate us in age. California girl, and Lord knows what kind of girl on my end. But there's fate for you. Hits you upside the head with one surprise after another. And fate was good to me. It handed me a friend. She is this calming, connecting force. She is present and real. She's what you might call one mother-lode of a righteous chick. And I love her. She'll be my friend for life. Of that, I'm certain. Geography, is incidental.

It's not all moonlight and roses. Scrapbooking gives us the opportunity to explore every facet of our lives. My life is charmed, but I'm not perfect. I choose to create pages about my less than stellar traits for two reasons: first, self-discovery comes from self-examination. Writing about my shortcomings can help me to work towards becoming a better me.

Second, I want my children to know I'm human. It may be several years, perhaps not until they're grown, that I'll share this page with them. My hope is that they might connect one day when they're parents themselves, realizing that we all do the best we can with each day we're given. Hey, just because you're all grown up doesn't mean you automatically have all the answers.

There are days when, for lack of a more eloquent word, I basically suck. Sorry, but it's true. It's never been easy living with the swirling pool of emotional highs and lows that make me who I am. I've learned to ride it, and for the most part, make it work. Some say it's the temperamental artist in me. My parents would say it's "pulling a Sarah Bernhardt." I might say it's me in all of my childish, self-centered glory. Whatever you call it, it means I yell over spilled chocolate milk. Or the sound of the kids playing is one decibel too loud. Or the counter has one too many piles on it. Or the endless requests and demands leave me wanting to climb into bed, pull the covers up tight, and drift away into a place that is much calmer…much less like me. | I often wonder if God's plan was for me to be this person—someone who often teeters on the edge of the next big meltdown, given the requisite variables. Or if this is simply my will getting in the way of some other, much more evolved, selfless being. I don't really know. I just know that there are days when I'm less than stellar as wife, a parent and a friend. It's not a reflection of my love or passion, it's just a sign of my shortcomings. As long as I can see that, I can work toward finding a better balance, and a better me.

MAR 14 2004

life's journey

DAYS

What about your relationships? A news flash: there is more to scrapbook than the lives of your kids! They make perfect subjects, but what about the other relationships in your life? Your parents? Your siblings? Your friends? All of these people should be in your scrapbooks. If you don't feel comfortable creating a page about yourself, then make a layout about your relationships with others. That way, you'll manage to include yourself in a roundabout way.

Ideas for scrapbooking friends

- how did you meet?
- what was your first impression? did it hold up over time?
- what connects you?
- how would he or she describe you?
- the things you admire in them

when we became three

It happened in the blink of an eye...okay, it actually took 9 months, and a couple of years of figuring out when in the world we'd ever be ready or capable of bringing a child into the world...and then, you were there.

Even as you grew inside of me, I had to wonder, "What is it going to be like having someone else live in my house?" For six years, Daddy and I had been plugging along, ironing out wrinkles along the way, as we learned to live together. You were the wild card—the third piece in the family puzzle. For some reason, it struck me as the trickiest part to becoming a parent—having to share my space with another living being. Forget about round the clock feedings and sleepless nights. I was about to get a new roommate.

But when we became three, the stars aligned. The mystery dissolved and the doubt fell away the minute I saw your beautiful face. It was my science experiment gone wonderfully, blessedly right. It wasn't only you born that day, sweetie. It wasn't only you.

start with the story

Sometimes, a thousand words can be worth a picture.

If you tend to leave your journaling to the end, try a different approach: write first. Before you even pick up a sheet of cardstock and begin to design, sit down in a quiet place and put your thoughts down on paper. Ninety percent of the time, I write first. Why? To ensure that my words will find the room they need to tell the story.

Start with the story. You may be surprised at how much (or how little) you write when the limits of space have been removed from the equation.

the **quest** for the **perfect pigtails**

Aidan definitely drew the short stick when it comes to moms who know how to create adorable, girlie looks for hair. Let's face it, my hair is an inch long on an average day, and the only skill I have is that of liberal product application. So whenever Aidan asks for pony or pig tails, I am instantly aware of my severe inadequacies. Sure, I see so many little girls out there with braids, or beads, or curls, and I stare at them with my jaw agape, scratching my head, and thinking, "Huh?" This photo was taken after a particularly proud moment in my hairstyling history. I am most proud that the part is just shy of completely centered and straight. And so, the quest for the perfect pigtails continues.

just give it **time**

The other day you asked when you could have a play date at Duncan's house. I told you, "Honey, you have to be invited over to have a play date." And with the most sorrowful little voice I've ever heard come from you, you sadly replied,

"But no one ever invites me over."

Oh honey, give it time. You are four years old, and you have stayed home with me since the day you were born. You haven't had a chance to make a social network like your sister did. I know it's hard to watch her go on all of her play dates. Just hold tight, sweetie. You are the coolest kid I know. You will have more friends than you can shake a stick at. Just give it time. APRIL 2004

Tell story, find photos. Because I scrap more moments than events, I'm faced with a recurring problem: most of the "moments" I want to scrap don't have photos that directly correspond to the story. When I had the above conversation with my son (one that broke my heart for a split second), I didn't have actual shots of him talking to me. But this exchange had to be documented. So I jotted down what

he said, and the next time I set out to scrap I found some random, unrelated portrait shots I had recently taken, and I used them on this layout. When you have a compelling story, the photos are really secondary. You have permission to use pictures that don't sync with the actual words. Don't let the rich moments of your life slip away because you don't have the photos to match!

You know how little kids will bring any type of life form home they can dig up and announce defiantly, **"I'm keeping him"**? Well, sometimes that's how I feel when I look at you. You're my little love pet. And really, you're not that different than a puppy. Here's how I figure it:

you are soft and cuddly

you aren't potty trained

you have sharp teeth (we plan to nip this in the bud)

you'll fall asleep anywhere

you tear around like a banshee

you make growling sounds

you know how to get what you want with those eyes

Yeah. It's official. I'm keeping you.

• i'm keeping him •

talk to me

The best way to become a better writer is simply to write more. And when you write, pretend as though you are sitting across from a dear friend, casually, intimately and truthfully giving him or her an account of your story. What would you say if you were showing pictures to your best friend? Wouldn't your tone be more relaxed and informal? That's exactly how your writing should sound.

Keep it conversational. Don't be afraid to be honest. On the flip side, don't feel as though you have to come up with artificial mush if it doesn't ring true for you.

Another secret to better and more meaningful writing is to start using the word "I" more often. Injecting your perspective will enliven everything you write. Go beyond the facts and ask yourself, "How did it make me feel? My reactions? How does seeing my children from a distance, walking side-by-side, affect me?"

By including your own perspectives, emotions or reactions to events and moments, you are enriching the story ten-fold—you're adding a piece of you to the process. Not only will your family members remember themselves better, but they'll also have a little more of you.

Seeing the two of you walking together down the streets of Madison made me keenly aware that you are both these completely separate little people from your Dad and I. As you walked, and I snapped away, I found myself getting a bit sentimental—will you stay side-by-side through-out your lives, giving each other support and encouragement in hard times and good? Will you maintain a sense of fun and adventure? Will you even talk to each other when you are teenagers? We love you both so insanely, and nothing makes us smile more than the two of you, spending time together, making each other smile. I hope you will always walk together, as siblings, but more importantly, as friends.

walking
in madison

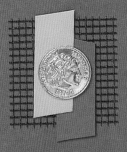

MAR 0 7 2003

Keep a writer's notebook. Buy yourself a pretty journal, something that speaks to your artistic, scrapbooking soul—and then use it! A writer's notebook is a great place to jot down:

- crazy, funny, adorable things your kids say

- subject ideas for layouts, along with notes on what you might want to say

- creative freewriting sessions

- the things you are grateful for, everyday

- a simple recounting of the day's events

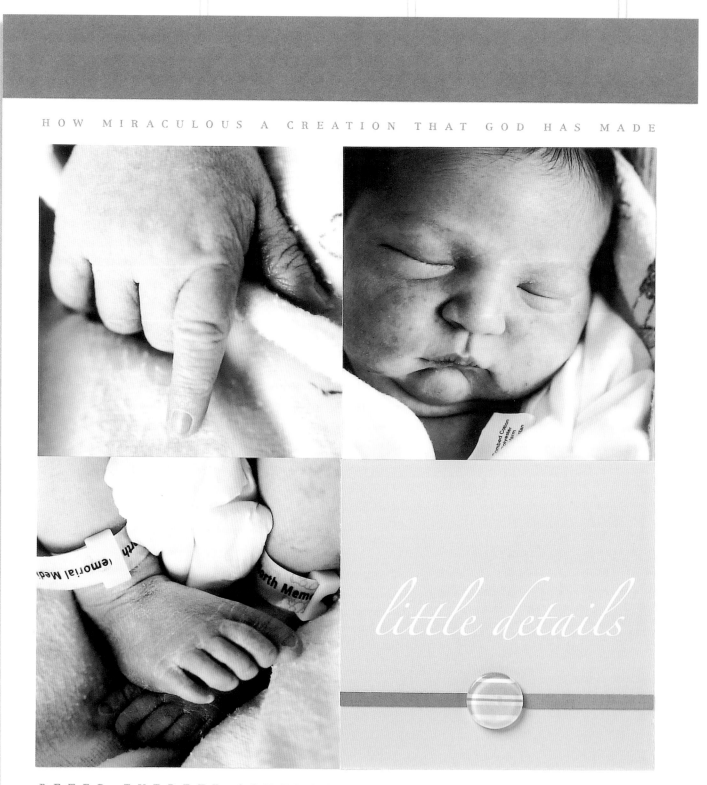

little details

chapter four

point & shoot

If there were support groups for Rabid Scrapbook Mom
Photographers Anonymous, I would be my chapter
president! I'm a camera-totin', picture lovin', portrait-
takin' fool. My children will likely need camera therapy
from all the times I've posed them. But at least they'll
have great photos to show their therapists.

Photography is my passion, and the reason I got
into scrapbooking. It allows me to freeze moments in
time, illustrating how I remembered those moments.
Or sometimes, how I thought I remembered them.
Frequently, I find that the photograph transcends the
moment and transforms the memory into a little
piece of magic.

**Anyone can learn to become a better
photographer.** I'm a little more proficient with
each roll I shoot. And believe me, I shoot a ton.

Be forewarned: I am not a professional photographer.
What I am is a slightly obsessive hobbyist who knows
how to focus and use my camera's program mode to
its fullest extent!

The urge to create, the urge to
photograph, comes in part
from the deep desire to live with
more integrity, to live more
in peace with the world, and
possibly to help others to
do the same.

—Wynn Bullock

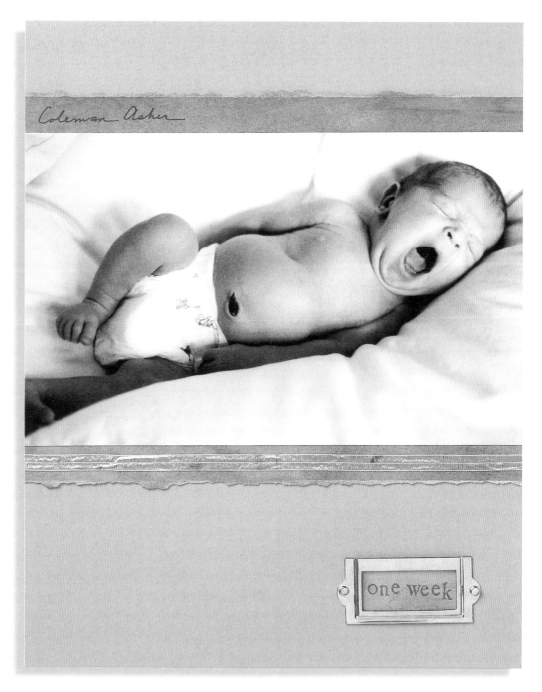

Coleman Asher

one week

myth vs. reality

The myth: You grab the camera, point and shoot, and keeping your fingers crossed you hold out hope that you captured the magic exactly as you saw it.

The reality: You realize you didn't see Grandma's elbow sticking into the shot of the new baby, or all that clutter in the background that detracts from the subjects. Or the shot wasn't in focus. Or the light was bad. The list is endless.

I'm right there with you. I shoot incessantly, just to get the three or four shots that sing to my photographer's soul. Even though shooting frequency is not a problem for most scrapbookers I know, keep reminding yourself: you can't just shoot a few shots here and there and expect to get what you're looking for. In this chapter, I'll share tips on how to take better pictures, regardless of camera type. Think of it as Photo Theory 101.

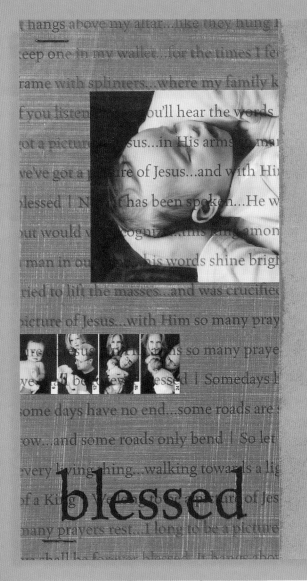

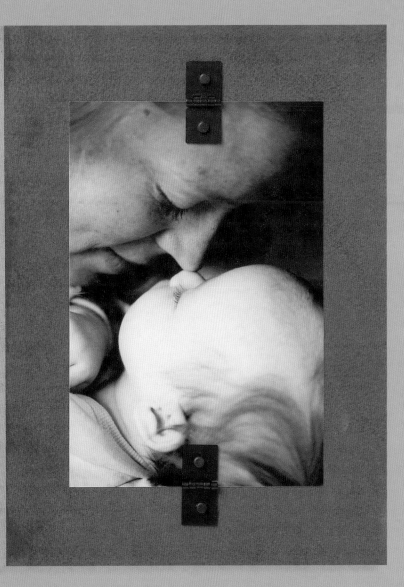

My photo toolbox

- Nikon N80 SLR camera body

- Nikon D70 SLR digital body

- 50mm Nikkor lens, 1.8

- 28-105 Nikkor zoom lens, 4.5

- 70-300mm Nikkor zoom lens, 4.5

I use a 35mm outfit for the interchangeable lenses. Almost every photo in this book was taken with my N80 body. I recently picked up a digital 35mm camera, and am still in the "getting-to-know-you-stage." (See p. 85).

I shoot exclusively in "program" mode. It keeps things simpler. Today's 35mm cameras make getting a good exposure almost foolproof. The word "almost" should be stressed!

love \ˈləv\ *n* 1 : cherish 2 : to feel a devotion or tenderness for 3 : a beloved person

my heart

composition

Whatever type of camera you own, a true under-standing of composition will improve every shot you take. You just have to learn to start seeing the shot through the lens. You can do this with a little patience and practice.

Once you start framing your shots through the lens, you'll end up with more and more usable pictures—ones that don't require any cropping!

Shot check

A few things to keep in mind when you're looking through the lens:

- Make a quick four-corner frame check. Look at each corner of the shot through the lens. Are you including everything you want? Are there distracting elements in your vision field?

- Horizontal or vertical? Which is best for the content you're shooting?

- Is there enough light on your subject?

- Are you too far away? Too close?

- Are you composing shots with the Rule of Thirds in mind?

The Rule of Thirds

If you want to take better pictures, you need to embrace the rule of thirds. The rule of thirds divides a shot into segments, based on two vertical and horizontal sets of intersecting lines. (See diagram below.) When you compose a shot, you should strive to have what you are shooting fall at some or all of the intersecting points.

When shooting portraits, eyes are a natural element to have land at these cross-sections, as seen at right. Below, note how my daughter's head and hands alight on intersecting points. The result: a more dynamic, engaging picture.

Circles mark areas of compositional emphasis. Shots that place the subject at any one of these intersecting points will have more impact.

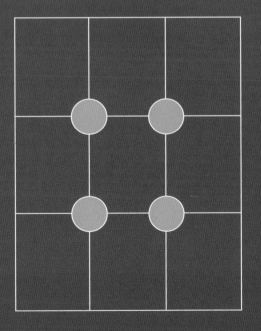

sassy \sas-e\ adj. 1. to be impudent, saucy. 2. vigorous and lively. 3. distinctively smart and stylish. 4. Aidan Isabella Zielske.

Sass? Yep, you got it kid. You come by it honestly, as they say. Some call it spirit; we just call it plain old sass. Sass is good. It will make you interesting. It will draw people to you like a magnet. Use it well, and only to charm, never to harm. It is a gift from God and is just one of the many facets of who you are.

JUN 02

To shoot this portrait, I used side lighting from a floor-to-ceiling kitchen window.

she's got the whole world, in her hands

look for the light

Natural light is a photographer's best ally. Yes, there are times when a flash is necessary to capture the action you're documenting, but with portrait-style photography, a flash has no business being on. None.

Indirect light from a window will give you the interplay between light and shadow that adds depth and texture to a photograph. I shoot every portrait I create

with window light. Even on an overcast day, you can have still have enough light to have a properly exposed frame.

Go from room to room in your home. Take test shots to get an idea of where the light is best. Shoot with a film speed of 400 or higher to minimize underexposure and blur.

Studio Secret Some studio! A messy bedroom with a piece of black velvet tacked onto a wall is the setting for the shot at right. The location doesn't matter as long as there is light.

catchlights

A literal example of seeing myself in you. December 2002

Catchlights are the reflection of light in a subject's eyes. Every photo enthusiast I know strives to capture as much reflected light as possible. In order to achieve this effect, be sure your subject is facing a strong, but indirect light source. Turn off the flash and shoot. If you look closely, you can see me in her reflection. Catchlight-o-licious!

She is a new friend for me...well, not so new now, but she is a gift. We met because of our mutual love and obsession for scrap-booking. She is funny, with the most infectious laugh of anyone I know. She is grounded and yet manic enough to relate to me perfectly. When I go to her house, I feel like I'm at someone's house who I've known for my entire life. She has a beautiful family, chock full of people with more personality than you can shake a stick at. She is honest and kind and fun. She has faith in God that is an inspira-tion, and it shows in all she does. I'm so blessed to have a friend like Margie.

my friend

home-made portraits

I stopped taking my daughter to a portrait studio when she was two years old. I was tired of getting the same old shots every six months. Nice enough to share with Grandma, but less than inspiring from a scrapbooking perspective.

You can take your own portraits! You'll need a camera that allows you to get in close for the shot, natural light, and a faster film speed.

The basics

- **A neutral backdrop.** Shoot against a plain wall, or throw a sheet up behind your subject. My favorite backdrop is a few yards of black velveteen.

- **A light source.** Ideally, you'll want natural, indirect window light. I always set my shots up within a few feet of a window that allows in plenty of indirect light. Watch out for direct sun streaming through. It will cause harsh shadows to fall on your subject.

- **400-speed film.** Color, or black-and-white, it's your choice! (My bias tends toward the latter.) Using film with an ISO of 400 or higher will work in most well-lit, natural light settings.

Closer, please...closer

While scrapbooking gives us endless choices when it comes to cropping photos, why not try removing the post-crop from the process? Use the pre-crop!

When shooting portraits, cut off part of the head before you shoot. With portraits, the tighter you crop in on a subject's face, the more dramatic the result. Unless you really need the subject's hair, go ahead and get close!

There really isn't anything more interesting than human faces, especially those mugs we love. If your focal depth allows it, fill that frame with a fabulous face and shoot away.

beautiful

in every single way

No-flash zone!

If you want to replicate the type of portrait shots you see here, the flash has to go! Flash lighting delivers a flat, even light that erases all of the subtlety and nuance achieved through ambient lighting.

A few other tips

Don't forget to change your subject's position, as well as the angle from which you're shooting. Do some straight-on, and some from a higher vantage point. Additionally, ask your subjects to remove their jewelry. I didn't do that here. A good example of do as I say, not as I do!

s i s t e r

s i s e

ellie and claire • december 2003

she will make you laugh, and sometimes cry

she will be willing company, and at other times,
completely in the way of everything you do

she will keep your deepest secrets, and yet still manage
to embarrass you in front of your friends

she will exclude you from things, yet be there
unsolicited at the times you need her most

she will be the truest bond you'll ever know

i'm gonna watch you

shine

MAR 2 0 2004

there will never be a father who loves his
daughter as much as I love you
—paul simon

posing your subjects

There are a few things you can do to improve how
your subjects look in the final shot.

- Arrange people's heads at different levels.
- Use simple props, such as a chair or stool.
- Have the subjects "scrunch" together right before
  you take the shot. The subjects actually might
  feel a little awkward holding certain positions
  or being that close, but on film the result will
  be more intimate and energized.
- Remember to shoot from different angles for variety.

going digital

I finally did it. I went digital. However, 97 percent of the photos
in this book were shot with my traditional 35mm camera. I'm
brand spanking new to the digital world, and have realized one
thing: I have much to learn! That said, here are some of the
advantages to going digital.

Instant gratification. I can take 145 shots of my son
attempting to tie his shoes, and I can see the images immediately! Digital frees you up to shoot as much as your memory
card can hold—and until you get the shot you're looking for.

Instant learning. For someone who shoots in program
mode, digital is giving me a chance to learn more about
photography. I can shoot with a million different settings
and see the results of my experimenting, without having to
pay to get the pictures developed.

Choices, choices. My camera shoots all photos in color,
and then I have the option to convert it to black-and-white. This
means I can have color or black-and-white on whatever photos
I want! No more switching film!

Digital is fun, freeing and fabulous. There are cameras available
in almost every price range as well. The more I play with mine,
the more I know it was meant to be.

Instant studio!

A sterile, painfully unadorned hospital room served as the perfect impromptu studio for my girlfriend, Marjorie, and Peter, her new baby boy. When I walked into the room, I saw a window. It, some tight cropping, and a little ingenuity are really all you need to create a memorable portrait. I simply made sure that Marjorie was turned toward the light enough, and I shot away.

It's all about light, composition and a little experimentation to find the best pose for your subjects. And it never hurts to carry a few spare yards of black velveteen in your camera bag!

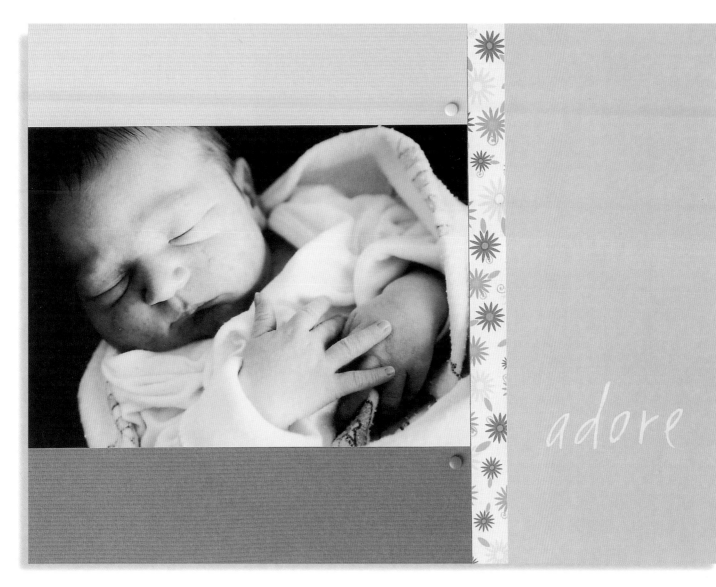

Highlight beautiful pictures with simplicity.

Simple layouts let beautiful photographs shine. I tried several variations on both of these before I decided to just use a simple color-blocked approach with minimal embellishments. The color combination is fresh, adding a hipness to the overall feel, but the execution is just clean and simple.

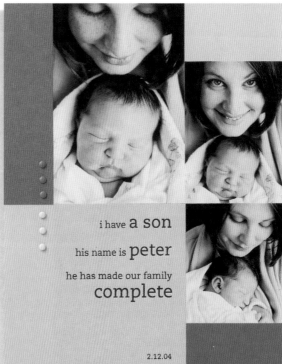

i have a son

his name is peter

he has made our family complete

2.12.04

The best $14.95 I ever spent

You know how usually, when you leave Target, and you're loading up your trunk in the parking lot, thinking, "What in Heaven's name did I just spend $75 on?" Well, this was not the case with one of the smartest purchases I've made to date: the Woody costume. Yep. That's where me and buyer's remorse will never cross paths. Cole has had more fun with that silly get-up than anything I can think of. I don't know if I should be concerned that it still fits him two years past the purchase, or happy. Either way, if his growth remains at its current rate, this thing might just make it to Halloween 2004. I may not need 20 rolls of paper towels, or that box of Krispy Kremes, but I know that Target costumes definitely have some staying power.

start 'em young

What kind of birthday party do you throw when your mother has every scrapbooking product known to woman? A scrapbooking party, of course! For Aidan's 8th birthday, we decided to have a scrapbook party. We told all the girls to bring three to five snapshots for our project. The theme of our little albums was "All About Me." It was so cool to see the girls get into it. Aidan was more excited about getting to the present opening than anything. And as usual, when you get six eight-year-olds together, they ended up making a haunted house in Aidan's room, and arguing a lot. Another happy birthday has come and gone!

everyday snapshots

I have a million snapshots, and I don't know what to do with them. Okay, it may not be a million, but I don't just take black-and-white portraits.

Maybe you're thinking, "Forget about artsy portraits; I just need to take better snapshots." I'm right there with you. Candid, everyday shots are, I believe, the hardest to take and take well. I do shoot two rolls at every birthday and holiday, but my results are usually less than stellar. And because I only scrap the pictures that inspire me, some of these events just go unscrapped. And that's okay.

But there are a few things to keep in mind to improve the scrapability of your everyday shots.

- **Shoot without a flash.** When you're indoors with enough light and a fast enough film speed, try leaving the flash off.

- **Close-ups and details.** When shooting any event such as a birthday party, don't forget to get some close-up shots of the birthday person, as well as some detail shots of the event: the cake, the candles, or the party activities. Doing this will give you options for focal point shots, as well as photos that provide a quick look at all the details.

- **Don't forget composition.** Remember to see the shot through the frame, and try to eliminate distracting background information when possible.

everyday magic

A day at the park yielded nothing spectacular, photographically speaking. A bunch of shots of the kids, swinging, running around—everyday-kids-at-the-park stuff.

I wasn't particularly motivated to scrap the photos. (Can you relate?) But as I flipped through the stack of photos a second time, I paused on the shot at right. It wasn't a particularly perfect or magical shot, but as I looked at it, I somehow knew it could be—with a little tender loving care.

So I scanned it into Photoshop, enlarged it, and converted it to black-and-white. And when I looked at the result, I knew exactly what I was going to do with and say about this shot.

It made me realize that sometimes you have to look a little deeper and realize that a snapshot can become magical—when you realize what you've captured. Upon closer examination, this photo says more to me about my son than a hundred paragraphs ever could. That's where the magic is.

Making enlargements

Scanning photos for enlargement is easy if you follow these simple steps in Adobe Photoshop.

1   Scan the photo in at 600 dpi or higher. You need the extra dpi, because you're going to change the resolution to increase the size of the photo.

2   Change the Resolution to 300 dpi. When you do this, be sure that the "Resample Image" box is unchecked. This will automatically increase the size of your photo while retaining print-ready quality.

3   Save the image as a TIFF.

4   Use the best quality, archival photo paper you can find. My favorite ink jet photo paper is Ilford Gallerie Professional.

5   Print out your enlargement on your photo printer. I have a Hewlett-Packard Photosmart 7960 that gives me really amazing results, especially on black-and-white photos.

so coleman

Something about this picture was so very four-ish to me—so very carefree, I-got-me-some-new-shoes-and-I'm-going-to-splash-in-some-puddles. But as I looked at it, I realized it is just so quintessentially you. Even though you have your rough-and-tumble moments, many of your habits are running slightly on the, dare I say, anal retentive side? It is so you to walk through puddles, but to be sure to pull your pants up so as not to get them wet. It's almost as if you're saying, "I'm a crazy four-year-old, but not that crazy." I love your orderly nature. I will always relate. The apple, my little buddy, doesn't usually fall too far from the tree. You keep tentatively splashing.

No one else would make more sense, or more insanity, or more fun, or more love.

Dan...Cathy...self-portrait...04

why black-and-white?

Give me a shot in black-and-white and I'll follow you anywhere. It's pure, truthful, artistic and engaging. Another reason I love to scrapbook with black-and-white photos is because color choices for cardstock and embellishment become wide open. I don't have to find the perfect pink to match my daughter's sweater, because it's only showing up in lovely shades of gray.

Black-and-white film removes all distraction and allows your subject to come shining through. Plain and simple. And black-and-white isn't just for special occasions or portraiture. I shoot it for birthdays, sporting events, Christmas—you name it! If you've never tried it, there is no time like the present.

New Year's Eve, 2002

night hockey

It's been a struggle with the mild winter of 2002, but Daddy has finally got the backyard rink fully fuctional. The kids got a chance to test it out on New Year's Eve. We had a small gathering of friends of family, and the kids bundled up and headed out to the rink. By the time these shots were taken, it was after 11 p.m. Nick is a real live hockey player, which was about the coolest thing in the world as far as Coley was concerned. Coley fell asleep immediately upon returning inside. Aidan the party girl, on the other hand, was up until 1:30 a.m.

smile

My favorite film. Although you can never beat the quality of true black-and-white film, I rarely shoot it. Instead, I opt for using color-processed black and white film. It costs the same to process as a regular roll of color film, and it gives you pretty accurate black-and-white tones. The key is to find a developer who can give you the most authentic-looking prints. I take all of my film to Wal-Mart, where they use a Fuji Frontier processing system. The results? As close to black-and-white as you can get without using the real deal!

AMA ZING

HOW DO YOU DO WHAT YOU DO

so much magic in your beautiful face

When I was six years old, I had missing teeth, bangs as crooked as the Mississippi River, and my Sears Toughskins made me the least fashionable kid on the block. When I see pictures of you like this, I'm honestly confused. Six-year-olds just aren't supposed to look this serene, this knowing, this together. I'd like to think it's from your fabulous gene pool, but somehow, I think it's something slightly more divine. Since the day you arrived, your Dad and I always felt you had an old soul—that you landed here with wisdom in tow. And I think that as you grow, we have come to believe this all the more.

6

chapter five
the art of type

I will never forget the **sublime moment** when, while playing around on that Macintosh in the University of Texas computer lab, I highlighted my name and changed the font from Palatino to Avant Garde. Eventually I changed the course of my professional career, making the leap from journalist to graphic designer. All on account of one thing, my absolute love of—and obsession with—computer fonts.

Typography, as it's called, is an art form. Don't let anyone tell you otherwise. The simple process of selecting a typeface and putting it on your page puts the entire creative universe at your fingertips. (Well, at least the typographic universe!)

This is a **designer's perspective** on typography and how it can apply to your next scrapbook page.

If I had a font for every photo...
            wait, I probably do have
a font for every photo.

—Cathy Zielske (ha!)

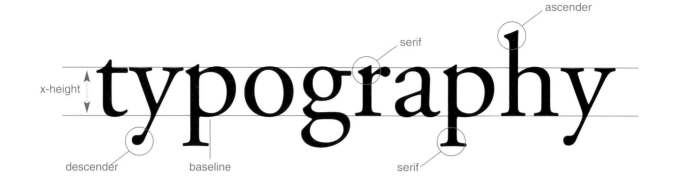

typography

labels: ascender, serif, x-height, descender, baseline, serif

serif   **sans serif**   *script*   **DISPLAY**

Adobe Garamond   Arial   Dearest Script   Dynamoe Hard

type basics

A little typographic knowledge can go a long way when deciding upon which faces to use on your next scrapbook layout. While typography can be broken down into numerous subcategories, I'm focusing on four groups for our purposes: serif, sans serif, script and display.

By examining the differences and personalities of type, you can make better choices when choosing faces for your pages.

But beyond "this is a perfect girlie font" or "this is the hands-down choice for birthday pages," I want to share a designer's approach to type, to empower you to make choices based on typographic theory. Further, while technically there are no real rules to scrapbooking, there absolutely are rules for typesetting. We'll explore some of the essential guidelines for better-looking type.

In this chapter, I'll use the terms "font," "face" and "type" interchangeably.

the photo

Taken on that fateful Labor Day weekend—love's point of no return, as you recall—this was the photo that introduced everyone else in my Texas world to Daniel Ezekiel Zielske. I adore this photo. And why wouldn't I? Look at how hot this man is! I remember pinning it on my bulletin board at work and gazing lovingly at it every two to three minutes all day long. One of my co-workers stole the photo after hours, scanned it, and turned it into a "Wanted: Dead or Alive" poster. Funny stuff. I still can't believe sometimes that now, 13 years later, it all worked out so amazingly well. And he's still totally hot.

Favorite Serif Fonts

• Adobe Garamond

• Times New Roman

• Janson

• PMN Caecilia
  (a slab serif)

serif type

Serifs are the angled, thick or thin swashes on letterforms. Generally speaking, serif faces are among the easiest to read. This is due in part to familiarity. Most of the body copy we read in books, magazines and newspapers is set in serif typefaces.

Serif faces aren't as flashy as some of their sans serif cousins. The beauty here is that serif faces often provide nice support to your photos and design, never calling too much attention to themselves. They are, by and large, the least trendy choices you can make. What does this mean for you? A layout that will not feel somehow dated.

Favorite Sans

Serif Fonts

• Zurich

• Universe

• Gill Sans

• Helvetica

• Bell Gothic

isn't she lovely?

isn't she wonderful?

our girl at eight

sans serif type

Sans serif faces do not have the extra swashes and details of serif type. The letterforms tend to be even in width and structure. If serif faces are the basic black dress of type, the sans serif (literally, "without serif") are the smart bag and matching shoes. They can go almost anywhere on a layout. They are comfortable in the cleaner, more graphic feel that is contemporary design, yet they remain neutral enough to avoid upstaging photos on a layout.

Carpenter
• CK Cursive
• Dearest Script
• Zapfino

A TRUE DIMANT'S GIRL

bubbly & frilly

ELENA AT SIX MONTHS

script type

Admit it. You love script fonts! They are luscious, elegant and decorative. Perfect for layouts about weddings, new babies, graduations and the like. Script fonts are like formal wear; you only pull them out on certain occasions that truly call for the extra ornamentation.

Use them sparingly—titles are an obvious placement—to enhance readability. The key here is restraint.

One word of caution: script faces are more challenging to read, and are therefore not the best choices for journaling blocks.

CANADA BEAR

HOW YOU CAME TO LOVE YOUR LITTLE OBJET DE COMFORT

He came from Canada. I think he did anyway. He came in a little gift bag from a CKU I taught at in Vancouver. So actually, he probably isn't legitimately from Canada, but...he has become your most treasured comfort object. Why you latched onto him so quickly, I know not. But I do know that Canada Bear, as he has come to be known, must be present and accounted for each night before you can fall asleep. Many a night has evolved into a massive search for Canada Bear when he goes AWOL. But we never fail to find him, and you never fail to fall soundly asleep with him nestled safely in your arms. I wonder how many years he will share your pillow. I remember my own comfort objects and how much they meant to me. Here's to many more years with Canada Bear.

display type

Display fonts, also called decorative fonts, are the catchall category of funky type. Anything that falls outside of the three previous categories is generally considered display. All of those shabby, grungy fonts? Group them here.

Here, in the Display type family, lurks notorious flavor and frivolity. If you're looking for a font with personality galore, display is your ticket. Note: display faces generally make poor choices for journaling, simply because of the inherent detail they possess.

Favorite Display Fonts

- DYNAMOE HARD

- 1942 Report

- TWO PEAS TASKLIST

- Garamouche

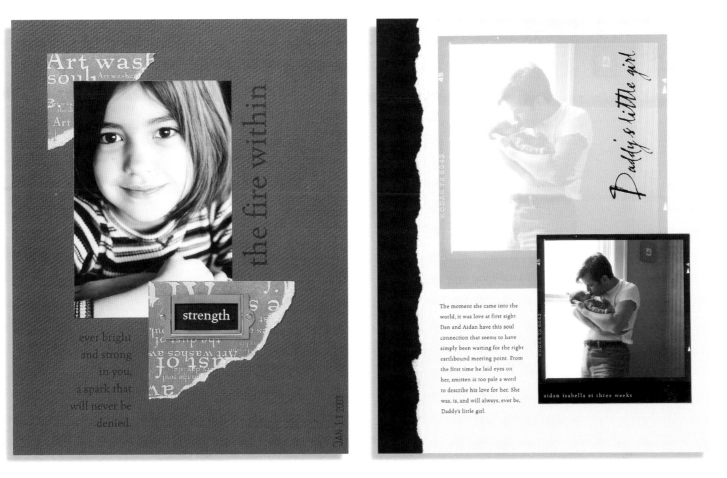

Art was
soul. Art washes
Art

the fire within

ever bright
and strong
in you,
a spark that
will never be
denied.

strength

JAN 11 2003

Daddy's little girl

The moment she came into the
world, it was love at first sight.
Dan and Aidan have this soul
connection that seems to have
simply been waiting for the right
earthbound meeting point. From
the first time he laid eyes on
her, smitten is too pale a word
to describe his love for her. She
was, is, and will always, ever be,
Daddy's little girl.

aidan isabella at three weeks

Can you identify the font categories?

**SNAP
SHOTS**

These days, I have to take what I can get when
trying to get you to hold still long enough for
a photo. I think it's just a reflection of what you
are right now—gregariously and constantly in
motion. I still think you're the cutest little boy
in the world. And as you know, the camera
never lies. So here's the proof.

APRIL 2003

f a c e s

2002

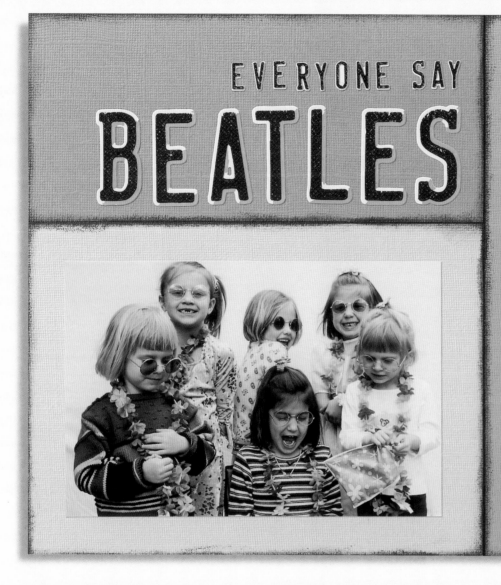

EVERYONE SAY **BEATLES**

I couldn't help myself. All those little girls in John Lennon glasses. Aidan's 6th birthday party had a theme, but you'd never know it by looking at these pictures. It was actually a "Garden Party." Yes—a garden themed party in March, when nary a green thing can be found.

Our birthday project was to paint pots and plant flowers. It went off without a hitch. Those girls sat so silently while they worked, I'm not even sure they were aware it was a "party." It was almost eerie!

Following cake and festivities, I shuffled everyone out into the chilly, overcast afternoon for the requisite group shot. They donned their Hawaiian leis and John Lennon glasses while Daddy held a white sheet behind them for an impromptu studio setting. Everyone say Beatles!

Happy birthday, Boots!

rule one

Insert only one space after a period when typing blocks of text. I know, it goes against everything you learned in Typing 101, but you only need one.

Today's fonts are designed with proportionate spacing between letters, unlike the typewriters of yesteryear which assigned the same space to each letterform, regardless of the characteristics of the particular letter.

Two spaces create unnecessary and distracting gaps in blocks of type. Occasionally, there is a font that doesn't quite conform to this typesetting convention, but the majority do.

All magazines, books and newspapers adhere to this rule. Try it, and your text blocks will appear more refined and polished.

changes

My dearest Coley…I realized something today. I spend a lot of time documenting your quirks and traits, but not very much on the monumental changes you've gone through in your fourth year. It's that second child thing at work—I just let you grow as you will without fixating on every single cognitive or physical step forward. I realized I haven't made a layout about the fact that you can brush your own teeth, and dress yourself in the morning, buttons and all. Or that you know how to navigate Nickjr.com without my help. Or that you understand what the term "figure of speech" means. Or that you can tell a knock-knock joke that actually makes sense. Or that you can make Pop Tarts without any help. I think there is a small part of me that is overlooking the changes because I'm hanging on to your fourth year as long as I possibly can. You'll always be my baby, but every new change takes you one step closer to five, and six, and seven. I know—these changes are inevitable. But I'm just holding onto my baby as long as I can.

rule two

Use leading to enhance readability. Leading is the space between lines of text. The term "leading" goes back to the days when typesetters used metal type and placed strips of lead between the lines to create space.

Leading enhances readability. Journaling blocks with little or no space between lines are hard to read. Don't let good writing fall prey to poor typesetting!

A good formula for leading is to double your type size. For example, if your type is 11 points, your leading should be 22. The layout above is 11 over 24.

Custom Leading

You can set a custom leading in most word processing programs. In Microsoft Word, go to the Format menu and choose the Paragraph submenu. In the Spacing section, select "Exactly" and then type in your leading amount.

OKAY, JUST ONE MORE GIRLS!

It's happening again. I feel like the Britany Spears of amateur photography. Oops, I did it again. Camera overload. I got some great shots of the girls on this particular day, but when I saw this shot, I realized that Aidan is just a few years away from "scrapbooking mom photo therapy." You know, she'll sit on the couch, recount how she can't actually recall her mother's features because they were constantly obscured by the camera. My epiphany from seeing this shot? No, not "no more photo shoots," but maybe fewer and far between. Yes, I will slow down on the old "just a few more, kids!" Until I get that digital camera, of course. Then all bets are categorically off.

{PHOTOGRAPHER'S NOTE: STOP WHILE YOU'RE AHEAD}

rule three

Keep line lengths shorter. Most magazines and newspapers use short line lengths, because they're easier for the human eye to follow. When lines of text run the complete width of the page, they're harder to read.

Line length goes hand-in-hand with leading. The end goal is always readability. I usually keep my line lengths to four inches or less. Only occasionally do I break that rule, and when I do I make sure the leading and type size is large enough to be easily read.

The journaling block above is large, but by keeping my line lengths shorter it doesn't feel as intimidating to read.

quotable aidan

"Waa!"—said very briskly and sharply, whenever something doesn't go her way. Charming!

"God is going to be mad at you, Mom."—said very matter-of-factly to Mom, who accidentally took the Lord's name in vain.

"Did you know that Daddy has a girl-friend in another state?"—said late one night to a somewhat stunned Mom, during a girl-talk session.

(a)lways (a)idan

automatic toilets
Aidan has a terrible fear of automatically flusing toilets in public places. If there isn't an adult around to cover the wall sensor, she doesn't go.

cheetos
Aidan could live on Cheetos. We don't plan to see if it could truly work.

play dates
Aidan could have play dates every day if her mother could handle the stress.

volcanic eruptions
Aidan went through a small phase where she was seriously concerned that a volcano would erupt. We had to point out our thankful lack of active volcanoes in the great state of Minnesota.

six years old

rule four

Limit your number of fonts. Too many fonts spoil the layout. Three or less should be the rule. Two, even better. I propose that you can do many layouts with only one font, simply varying the size and weight of the fonts for contrast and variety.

Type should serve to support your theme, not dominate it. Therein lies the beauty of simple font application. You really don't need to know which fonts work together and which ones don't when you stay with a single face, right?

This layout uses one type face, Times New Roman, in regular and bold. Many fonts come in packages with varying weights. This is handy for creating seamless layouts with a single font, while still introducing variety.

e l i z a

at three

anything goes

come along

for the ride

OCTOBER 03

relationships

When you understand the basics of typography, you're ready for the next step: type relationships. There are two distinct ways that type can interact with itself and other faces.

Concord

Type is said to have a concordant relationship with the page when there is little contrast between the typographic elements. Unity is a key word here.

You create a concordant relationship when you use a single typeface. Even if you vary the size and weights of the font, the inherent unity in a single face is undeniable.

Concordant relationships are calming and supportive. They do not distract from the other visual information on the page.

This layout is one of the few computer-generated pages I've created. It's a lift of a Nike ad I saw in a design annual. I used varying weights of Helvetica for everything except the large "a", which is Celestia Antiqua. Using varying weights of a single type family will give your page a concordant feel without seeming boring.

when coley **ruled** the world

When Coley ruled the world? Funny, I wasn't aware his reign was over! Okay, so he's a bit of a little dictator of late, and his list of demands gets longer with each glass of chocolate milk. I like to think of his new era as the Flabbergasting Fours, twice-removed cousin from the Terrible Twos. I say, revel in your glory, little man. We can take it. Experience the never-to-be-felt-again power of four while you're there. My only sadness? You won't truly remember what it was like to rule the world. Here's to praying that you do. SUMMER 2003

Contrast

Remember talking about emphasis in the chapter on design? You can do the same thing with type. By choosing two typefaces that are dramatically different, or by using type sizes that are notably different, you create contrast on a layout.

Type becomes another embellishment on your layout when the contrast is high. It also adds to the overall visual interest of the page. It injects a little typographic drama and excitement.

This layout is an example of taking two different fonts and playing up the differences through size, color and overall type style. Notice that just a few keys words are made to stand out. If you make too many things stand out, you create a chaotic feel.

Use contrast to make one word stand out on the page, like "ruled" does here, or "cousins" on the facing page. Think of it as creating a focal point with type. One thing stands out above all others. Then you're on your way to creating strong contrasts with type.

It never fails. At every family event, we try in vain for the perfect cousins shot. Ranging in age from four months to 21 years, we always look to the big boys to set the standard. In other words, Matt, Jake and Nick hold onto the little ones and try to wrangle some cooperation out of them. And this shot is as good as it gets. Yep—pretty much priceless. CHRISTMAS 2003

attempting to shoot the

COUSINS

bedtime rituals

IMPORTANT NOTE: *Mom and Dad alternate bedtime duties each night. On occasion, they will deviate slightly from the established routine, most often in the form of the "story forfeit" for other favors, such as "I will forfeit stories to watch the end of this Disney movie." Please note: this always ends in disaster, because kids have a hard time accepting the forfeit they agreed to. Also, parents will occasionally barter for duty trade. Think "I scratch your back…" deal making. Or, if one parent is just too tuckered out, too stressed out, or just plain out, the other parent will do back-to-back nights.*

7 P.M.–8 P.M.
A last hour of cartoons. Usually, it's Nickelodeon. Spongebob is always a favorite. Even for adults.

7 P.M.–8 P.M
Last Chance for Snack (which is the official title). This is where Fla-Vor-Ice and Cheetos come into play. Coley usually opts for chocolate milk.

8 P.M.
Stories for Coley in Mom and Dad's bed. The tradition of two stories at bedtime continues. Coley usually requests one book, and one magazine culled from Dan's stack of *Sports Illustrateds*, *New Yorkers* and *National Geographics*. (We don't read the mags word for word. Think of it as creative paraphrasing.) Afterall, the *New Yorker* isn't really known for page after page of great pictures.

8:30 P.M.
Coley's bedtime. Coley gets tucked in with a nightly prayer, and a fresh sippy cup of water. We turn his nightlight on, leave his door wide open, and always leave the room with the same phrase: "I'll check on you in a little bit." Then it's onto Aidan's room. On an average night, he is asleep in minutes. Otherwise, he'll make numerous requests for fresh water, or the always hilarious, "Mom, clean my room!"

8:30 P.M.
Aidan's turn. Aidan will often choose a variety of different activities for her bedtime. It used to be stories, but since she turned 7, she likes to play two or three card games. Speed, 7 Card Stud, Go Fish and Slap Jack are her favorites. Prayers and hi-lo follow.

9 P.M.
Aidan's unofficial bedtime. Although we try to get the lights out sooner, this is often the time the switch is actually flipped. Then, whichever parent has bedtime duty will hang out in the office until Aidan falls asleep because she doesn't like to be upstairs all by herself. This can take anywhere from a brief 10 minutes to an hour, depending on how tired she is. We also leave Aidan's door wide open. Mom likes to say, "It's like we all share one big bedroom, so there's nothing to be afraid of." Yeah, *that's* convincing.

10 P.M.
Everyone is soundly asleep. Parents can actually sit and have a conversation, as long as one of them is still awake. Most often, it seems we spend the last hours of the day catching up on all the things we would have been doing during the bedtime hours—paperwork, laundry, freelance etc. But as tedious as the routine can be after a long day, I know we will remember them wistfully, one day soon.

A word about typos

Argh! It kills me every time! I finish a page and I'm sitting there, admiring it, when, inevitably, there it is—a typo!

Sometimes, I'll go back and change it, and sometimes I just say, "It's a scrapbook page, not a Master's Thesis!"

My point is this: I draw the perfection line at spelling. My family will be the only ones who knew Mom typed a little too fast and didn't use a spell checker, right? Yes, my family, and anyone reading this book…

all type

There is no written rule in scrapbooking that says you're required to put photos on every layout! Sometimes words are all you need. With no photos to consider, space for journaling is not an issue.

Take a favorite inspirational quote and give it a page all its own. Document your children's bedtime rituals, or your favorite musicians of all time.

Try to fill up a scrapbook page with words. Flex your typographic muscle!

…but the biggest mistake I made

is the one that most of us make while doing this.

I did not live in the moment enough

This is particularly clear now that the moment is gone, captured only in photographs. There is one picture of the three of them sitting in the grass on a quilt in the shadow of the swing set on a summer day, ages 6, 4 and 1.

and I wish I could remember

what we ate, and what we talked about, and how they sounded, and how they looked when they slept that night. I wish I had not been in such a hurry to get on to the next thing: dinner, bath, book, bed.

I wish I had treasured the doing a little more and the getting it done a little less. —anna quindlen

note to self: what's important…and why i scrapbook

JOURNEY
[the guilty
pleasure]

[TEARS FOR FEARS]

U2
[the best band
ever, next to
the Beatles]

[BAUHAUS]

[DURAN DURAN]

PETER
GABRIEL
[the perennial]

[JOE JACKSON]

MADONNA
[the even guiltier
pleasure]

THE
POLICE
[the trip down
memory lane]

[PRINCE]

R.E.M.
[the saving grace]

[DAVID BOWIE]

BEN
HARPER
[the current
big thing]

TOM
WAITS
[the acquired
taste]

THE MUSIC THAT MATTERED

Or rather, matters. Let's make that present tense. I've always taken music seriously. I recall desperately hoping beyond hope that I would get to meet Steve Perry one day. Or Sting. Or Peter Gabriel. Yes, it was idol worship, but with a noble purpose: to say thank you. Thank you for all that inspiration. And passion. And beauty. And brilliance. The music matters. It makes me soar, weep, dance, reflect, sing, dream, and rock and roll.

type process

So you're thinking, "Great, Cathy, now how do I make it look like you do?" This is where my love for all things simple gets a bit cloudy. For me, typesetting is painless, because I've been doing it for years in my work. And I use high-end desktop publishing programs, such as Quark Xpress and Adobe InDesign to create the type for my layouts.

But before you gasp at the sticker shock of those programs (both run around $800 or so), there is good news: just about everything you see can be created in Microsoft Word, or other comparable desktop publishing programs. Here are ways to recreate the type treatments you see throughout this book!

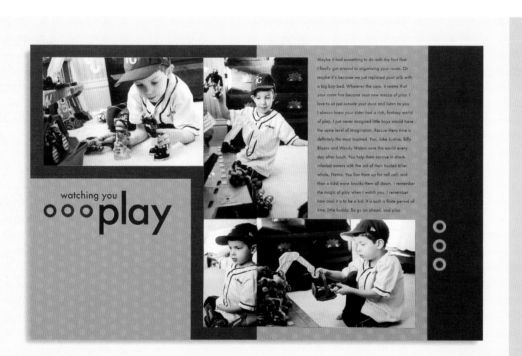

Getting type where you want it

The trick to getting your titles and journaling blocks where you want them is through digital sketching. You're already using your computer, right? All you need to do is measure your photos, then create text or picture boxes to serve as picture placeholders in your computer document. Place your photo boxes where you want them to appear on your final page. Now you can see exactly where to place your text boxes to hold your titles and journaling. Once you place them, then delete the empty picture boxes and print.

Be sure to print a test on plain paper to be sure you have things in the right place before running your cardstock through.

This approach takes practice, but once you start, you'll realize that it's simple to get your type exactly where you want it to be. See page 117 for more on digital sketching.

Create white type

Creating white type, or "reverse" type effects in Microsoft Word is simple.

* First, create a text box.

* Next, type your words.

* Using the fill option, choose a fill color for the background of your text box.

* Highlight your text and change the color to white.

Now you're ready to print out your reverse type on your color printer. You can trim it or punch it into shapes. Create individual letter blocks with colored background to create your own custom alphabet. Use a small circle or square punch to trim them out. For a seamless finish to a large block of color, print on semi-gloss photo paper.

handwriting

I can't apologize for loving fonts. They give me control, choice and endless creative options. I use computer fonts on almost every layout I create, mostly because I'm not crazy about my handwriting. It's not that I think it's horrible, but it doesn't give me the look I'm trying to achieve with most of my layouts. Further, it allows me to make sure I have room to say what it is that I'm trying to put down.

That said, I wouldn't deny the inherent emotional value of using your own hand on a page. When my children see my words written on a page, they're going to connect to every note they ever got written on a napkin in their lunch.

So, I keep trying to be happy with my writing. It's a work in progress. But until that time, bring on the fonts.

The same rules apply!

Even when you create layouts with your own handwriting, you can still apply typographic rules! For example, shorter line lengths will still be easier to read. Allowing for space between your lines of text will enhance readability. And, creating contrast between titles and journaling is as simple as writing bigger.

When I do use my handwriting, I like to use fun products like rub-ons or stamps to create my page titles. Maybe one of these days I'll try to write a fancy title in my own hand. No, actually, I won't. I just figured I should say that. Next topic…

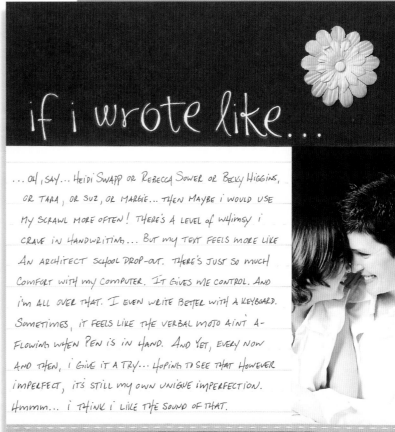

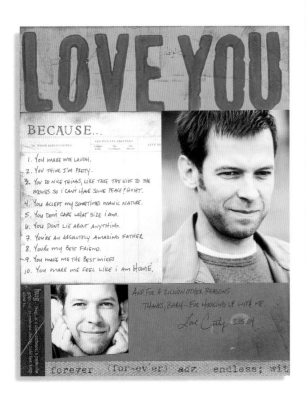

good things

REMEMBER

G

T

it's all good, baby. it's all good.

good

chapter six
simply inspired

How did I get involved in such a cool hobby? Was it luck? Fate? The newspaper article about the new scrapbook store that was opening in my hometown? Maybe it was a little of everything.

There's one thing I know for sure. Through scrapbooking we are creating lasting legacies to be enjoyed and shared. We are preserving the moments and events that matter most, and that make this life worth living. Honestly, though, my main motivation for scrapbooking? Scrapbooking makes me happy. Whenever I try to really delve into what it is that makes me adore this hobby, it always comes back to that. It makes me happy.

So if you want to take a peek into what makes me tick as a scrapbooker, read on. Just a few final bits and pieces from one clean and simple scrapper to you.

To live a creative life,
we must lose our fear
of being wrong.

—Joseph Chilton Pearce

my simple toolbox

I won't lie. I collect scrapbook supplies as if my life depended on it. However, I've come to realize that there are just a few things I really use on a daily basis These are the basics. If you took away my remaining trove of stuff, I could still create pages that would stand my personal test of time.

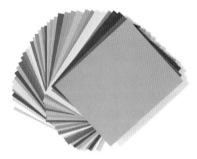

Cardstock

After film processing costs, I spend most of my scrapbook supply money on cardstock. All colors, all textures, in both 8½ x 11 and 12 x 12. I am a stay-at-home scrapbooker, rarely if ever venturing out to crops, so I'm always replenishing my stock to have the perfect sheet handy when I'm ready to go.

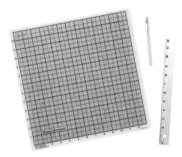

A cutting system

Every scrapbooker needs a trusted cutting system. For me, they're the old stand-bys: a large cutting mat, metal ruler and an X-acto knife. Paper trimmers offer a much simpler approach than this; I just never learned how to use one.

Repositionable adhesive

A repositionable adhesive, such as Hermafix, is probably my favorite of all scrapbooking tools. Why? Because if you don't like where you put something down, or, if you realize it's crooked beyond belief, you just lift it off and try again. Absolute genius, right?

A computer

Okay, a computer is far from a "simple" tool. I use my computer for creating titles, journaling, and embellishments; for making photo enlargements; and even for "sketching" out page layouts ideas. (See facing page.)

Those are the basics. But if I had to name a few more items that all scrapbookers, especially those who are new to the hobby, could add to their stashes, these would include:

- An assortment of patterned papers that appeal to your personal taste and style
- A black or brown pen for journaling
- A couple of stamp ink pads in brown and black
- An alphabet stamp set
- Glue Dots, fabulous for adhering anything with a little more weight
- Foam tape, for adding subtle depth to elements on a page

there's something about # Apple

We met for the first time in the University of Texas computer lab. The year was 1989. Me, and the little beige box with the 9-inch screen and the sweetest little icons you ever saw…the Macintosh. It was love at first byte.

My only experience with computers up until that point were the silly classes I took in high school, where line A equaled line C, or something like that. Now, in front of me, was this intuitive little charmer that would change my life forever. And the cool thing was that you didn't have to know a thing about computers to make them really work!

Apple empowered people to be the best they could be. How else can you explain a girl with a journalism degree eventually becoming an art director.

I will never forget my first Macintosh. The IIsi. It was a beautiful, beige, pizza box, and it came used without a hard drive, but I didn't care. I had a Mac of my own. I kept on purchasing new Macs to keep up with my ever-growing demands, but I didn't stop there. I also invested in an iBook for all of my teaching needs, and last spring, bought an iPod for Dan, as a present for finishing his first marathon.

Yes…there's just something about Apple. I'm sure PC users appreciate their machines too, but Apple users are just a little bit different—they actually love their computers. When you walk into an Apple computer store, you almost feel this glib, all-knowing connection to everyone there. Yes… I have a Mac, too.

So thank you, Steve Jobs, where ever you are…

working with computers

From creating titles and journaling blocks, to planning how my pages might come together, my Mac is with me every step of the way.

Digital sketching helps me to know exactly how everything will fall into place. By creating graphic boxes that are the same size as my photos, I get an accurate visual reference of what my page is going to look like. It also helps me know where to place my text and journaling so I don't have to waste sheet after sheet of paper trying to get my type in the right place.

I use Adobe InDesign, a desktop publishing program, but you can use basic word processing applications, such as Microsoft Word, to create digital sketches like the one below. All you need to learn how to do is work with text boxes.

Further, my computer allows me control over my journaling. I can tweak point sizes and placement until I'm sure I have enough room for every word.

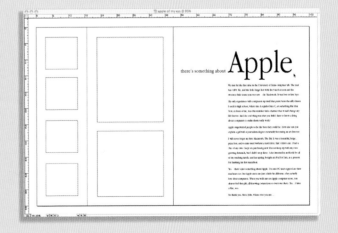

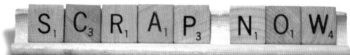

working spaces

Some scrapbookers are fortunate enough to have
a spare room in their homes to customize a little
scrapbooking Shangri-la of their own. Peace,
organization and sanity.

I am not one of those people.

What I have is a dining room. And no, you can't
eat there. You'd probably wind up with adhesive
in your food.

But guess what? You can be a scrapbooker, regardless
of what type of space you have to work in. I know
women who have a corner of their bedroom, or a few
drawers of space in their kitchens, and they still make
beautiful pages and have fun in the process. You just
have to scrap where you are.

There are so many amazing organizational products
designed for space-challenged scrapbookers, whether
you're a hard-core addict like me, or simply someone
who dabbles a little here and there.

Scrap where you are! My dining room is the perfect place to indulge in my craft. It's centrally located; I can dabble while keeping an eye on the kids; and nothing matches anyway, so, what's a few extra scrapbooking supplies here and there?

Now, even though I don't have a room of my own, I did find a way to customize the small space that I do have. Working with a furniture designer, I created a custom scrap cabinet. The cabinet, built from durable but inexpensive Melamine, cost me $650, but it is completely customized for the way I work and store my supplies. Inside are two removable paper storage units for my cardstock, and space for all of my other scrapbooking accoutrements. Inside my cabinet, you'll also find these:

- **Sterilite three-drawer containers**: perfect for storage of everything from stamps to punches. I have six of these and use them for everything.

- **12 x 12 plastic storage totes**: this is where I keep all of my patterned paper, stickers etc. The totes are clear and I can easily remember where I stored particular lines of paper.

- **Jars for ribbon storage**, tins for stamp storage and other little doodads.

- **A fishing tackle box**: it's been the ultimate storage lifesaver for all of my smaller embellishments.

Of course, you need a worktable. But really, any table will work. It doesn't have to be a dedicated scrap table. My 100-year-old dining room table, along with an oversized cutting mat, has served me just fine.

So do I still wish I had a room of my own? Um, yes. I do. Nevertheless, it's not going to stop me from finding creative solutions for working with the space that I have.

All I can say is thank goodness we have an eat-in kitchen.

1 Select photos...

Seems fairly obvious, right? The only time this step changes is when I know what I want to say before I have the photos.

...and journal

There are many times when I know what story I want to tell before I ever find the pictures to go with them. Or, if I know I have the photos, I'll just sit down at the computer and start to write before I do anything else. The story is as important as anything else on the page. I usually write first, and then proceed with building the layout.

2 Choose cardstock

Because I scrap black-and-white shots so often, this is the anything goes step. Whatever mood I'm in will dictate my color choices. I also have this fabulous color resource, *Color Index*, by Jim Krause. It offers more than 1,100 color combinations! It was created to help graphic designers specify colors, but it's an amazing resource for scrapbooking.

3 Design

Next, with photos in hand I sketch a rough idea on paper, or I go to the computer and create a digital sketch. I create text boxes roughly the size of my photos, place them in my document, and then start positioning words and titles around them. It gives me a quick visual check of how much space I have and how everything will fit together. Then I edit my journaling to fit, possibly eliminate non-essential photos, etc., until I feel the page is ready to be put together.

my process

Predictability. It's a key word to describe how I approach the creative process. My graphic design background doesn't hurt, either. I know how to get my titles and journaling where I want them, because that's what I've been doing professionally for the past 16 years. However, because I feel my words are just as important as a well-designed page, journaling first is one of my go-to approaches. Whether it's a few lines or several paragraphs, I'm always sure to have enough room to tell the story. Everything else can fall into place after that.

4 Test prints

I always print out my titles and journaling on plain white paper to check if where I've placed them will work with the photos.

5 Final production

When I'm sure everything will fall into the right place, I load my cardstock and print. Then comes the fun part: trimming, cropping and adhering.

IT'S A LONG WAY TO THE TOP IF YOU WANNA

ROCK & ROLL

And if AC/DC says it's true, you know there ain't no lyin'! Right now, Cole rocks. Literally. He is an insane, hard-rocking, 34-pound machine. He's been drawn to rock and roll for years—all four of them— but after seeing School of Rock, he's kicking into overdrive. No, not the Bachman Turner sort, but the heavy duty legends of rock featured on the film's sound track—AC/DC and Led Zeppelin. He is constantly rocking out. He makes all the sounds himself. He's either going to be the greatest rock musician of all time, or a great replacement for that sound effects guy in all those Police Academy films. What I love most about this new phase is that it reminds me of how much I love to rock. Artsy music is fine and dandy, but sometimes, the soul just needs a bass, a drum and a guitar. Cole's got this one figured out at an early age. He also has a series of names for his band: The Car Accidents, The Train Wrecks, and the Japanese Skeletons. And if he ever gets a mohawk or dyes his hair green, I swear I won't fight it. Because when you understand that what you look like on the outside has absolutely nothing to do with what's in your soul, then you're one step ahead. And that, my friends, rocks.

HAIR PRODUCTS WELCOME AND ENCOURAGED

YES TO MOHAWKS

NO BARNEY ZONE

REQUIRED LISTENING: AC/DC, LED ZEPPELIN, QUEEN, THE CLASH AND THE RAMONES.

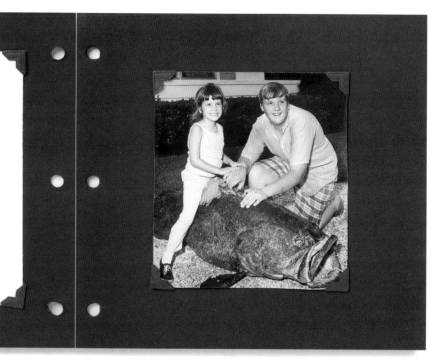

Little Cathy and Big Fish

JUNE 1970

I love this photo. Heck, I love any photos from my childhood, because to be honest, I don't have that many. I was four-years-old, and sitting on some big old fish caught by a neighbor. It was some record-setting size, so the newspapers came out for this shot. My mom tells me they had to do quite a bit of coaxing to get me on that big old slimy thing. She also reminds me the papers referred to me as "six-year-old Cathy MacDonald" in the cutline. They guessed my age, and my mom always said, "They think you're older because you're tall and well-spoken." Who can argue with that?

simple albums

For someone like me, who seems to have no rhyme or reason to my scrapbooks, simple theme albums have been an incredibly easy way for me to find a beginning, middle and an end.

Simple theme albums can be about anything you like, with the key being a single topic to focus on. Take for instance my "Photos I Love" album. I found my favorite photos of all time, used one shot for each spread, and journaled about why the photo was a favorite. Simple. And finished in a weekend.

Another favorite album is "My Happy Little Life." Once I decided upon a simple color scheme to use in my funky aluminum scrapbook, all I had to do was gather photos and create my journaling pages. I finished this album in one day.

Simple albums follow a format, which can include any or all of the following: title page, dedication page, contents page, section pages, and filler pages. Most of my simple albums just have a simple dedication and section spreads.

The key is deciding on your subject, choosing your papers, embellishments and design, and sticking to it. Before you know it, you've got a finished album.

This is a little book to celebrate and acknowledge all the things in this life that make me happy. While I have the tendency to complicate things, at the core, what makes me happy are the simplest of things...from a good supply of Fla-vor-Ice, to a clean kitchen. Simplicity is the key to happiness. And that doesn't mean you have to simplify your standards. It just means you have to keep it real. And what is real is what matters most. And what brings you joy. And what makes you happy. These are some of the things that make me happy. 3.22.04

introduction

Now I suppose this could go without saying, but I'm not leaving that one to chance! Dan, Aidan and Cole. That is happiness in a nutshell. Maybe because they are all so nutty in their own ways, but they make me happy. From the creative puppet shows to little notes and pieces of art created just for me, to everything else that makes up my life with these people. My family makes me happy. It all starts with them. Technically, everything else is superfluous. They are the base to the happy pyramid that makes up my life. No two doubts about it.

family

Scrapbooking magazines will always give you ideas to create the latest and greatest. This mini-accordion album was inspired by an article I read in a magazine.

simple inspiration

Inspiration is everywhere for scrapbookers. From the pattern on a rug in a Pottery Barn catalog, to a billboard you might see driving down the highway. You simply have to keep your eyes open and sketchbook handy.

But you want to know the best kept secret for great layout and color ideas? Graphic design books and magazines. Take a trip to your bookstore and find the graphic design section. There, you will find design annuals chock full of the most creative design work being done today.

Of course, other good resources are scrapbooking idea books, such as the one you currently hold in your hands. I buy pretty much every book that comes out, just to see what's cool and new in this hobby.

Adapting what you see doesn't simply mean direct lifting of layouts. Maybe it's a simple color scheme you want to copy, or the way someone has layered a tag with letter stickers and photos. You can pull out any element and adapt it to your own unique style.

And don't forget, you really do have your own style. Take everything you've gleaned from this book to make your own pages more representative of who you are as a scrapbooker.

And above all, have fun. It's the coolest hobby out there.

Graphic design annuals are one of the best resources for inspiration. From color combination to innovative page layout ideas, they offer a trove of cool, fresh and original ideas you can adapt. I love using design books because they will often push me outside of my box to try something different, like the layout at right. Stop by your local bookstore and browse away.

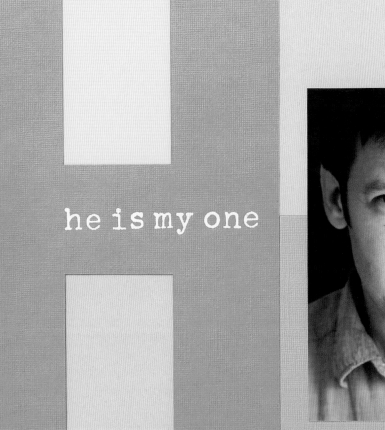

he is my one

Index

Index

Online Resource
Don't have friends who scrapbook?
Or maybe you're looking for ways to
connect with other people who share
your passion? Online scrapbooking
communities are a great way to meet
other scrapbookers, get ideas, and purchase all those fabulous products you
crave. Here are a few of my favorite
online scrapbook sites:

www.simplescrapbooksmag.com (ha!)
www.scrapsahoy.com
www.scrapvillage.com
www.twopeasinabucket.com